I0479706

SHUT UP
AND
DO IT!

SHUT UP
AND
DO IT!

PROPERTY INVESTMENT

My Side Hustle for Wealth and Security

ROHAN MANUEL

Copyright © 2021 by Rohan Manuel.

Library of Congress Control Number:		2021910325
ISBN:	Hardcover	978-1-6641-0579-9
	Softcover	978-1-6641-0578-2
	eBook	978-1-6641-0577-5

All rights reserved. No part of this book may be reproduced or transmitted in any form or by any means, electronic or mechanical, including photocopying, recording, or by any information storage and retrieval system, without permission in writing from the copyright owner.

Any people depicted in stock imagery provided by Getty Images are models, and such images are being used for illustrative purposes only.
Certain stock imagery © Getty Images.

Print information available on the last page.

Rev. date: 07/09/2021

To order additional copies of this book, contact:
Xlibris
AU TFN: 1 800 844 927 (Toll Free inside Australia)
AU Local: 0283 108 187 (+61 2 8310 8187 from outside Australia)
www.Xlibris.com.au
Orders@Xlibris.com.au
823493

CONTENTS

1   Introduction 1

2   Growing Up in the Australian Property Market 3

3   New, Off-the-Plan Build 11

4   Old Properties 18

5   Rural Properties 25

6   Principal-and-Interest versus Interest-Only Loans.............39

7   Apartments 41

8   Money Is Not a Dirty Word 44

9   Why Do People Invest? 48

10 Step 1: Budget and Finance 53

11 Cash Flow Positive 60

12 Negative Gear versus Cash Flow Positive 63

13 Mining Towns...65

14 Currency 73

15 Subdivisions 75

16 Relocated Homes 78

17 Land Banking 93

18 Funding 96

19 Step 2. Determine What Property and Location I Want 99

20 Step 3. Let's Make a Deal 101

21 Commercial Property... 105

22 Step 4. Buying the Property 110

23 Step 5. Running the Property.. 117

24 Where to Next? 122

1

Introduction

At the time I wrote this book, the world was in the grips of a pandemic. I live in Melbourne, which had one of the most stringent Covid-19 lockdowns in Australia. I watched as a number of friends and family members suffered job losses. Their superannuations and shares have diminished, and they are wondering what their next steps are. Will they be OK? What is the government doing to help them? I saw the government doing their best to provide support, handing out money it doesn't have to support people who are now without jobs and businesses that have had to shut down. This was done to protect people as much as possible and give the economy a chance to recover. The volume of debt that is being projected is around $1 trillion, which at best will take decades to repay.

Living in lockdown, unable to travel more than five kilometres and being under a curfew sounds like the start of a futuristic fictional novel, but it is currently life as we know it. However, it doesn't have to be all doom and gloom. I look at lockdown as a time when I can focus my attention. To that end, I have been working hard with real estate agents, banks, lending brokers, and accountants, and I just bought my seventeenth property. Yes, that's right—my seventeenth property.

I have been told that what I am doing is different from normal property investing. In fact, I have been called crazy. Maybe I am, but for me, crazy seems to be working. Some of the books I've read by Robert Kiyosaki, Warren Buffett, and Scott Pape about assets, value for your hard-earned money, and disciplined approaches suggest I'm not so crazy, after all. Or if I am, then I am in good company.

This book represents over twenty years of my experiences in the property market. My intent is not to give financial advice, nor am I telling you what you should do. I'm not trying to coerce you into following a particular strategy. I believe that you, the reader, are the only one who truly understands what is most important to you, and therefore, it is up to you to choose what you want to invest in. It is up to you to choose what you want to do with your money. It is up to you to choose how much you are willing to sacrifice. You must make up your own mind on what works for you.

I am writing this book, in part, to put down on paper my thoughts and experiences, in the hope that it will help my son and daughter understand what I've been doing for the last twenty years but also aid my friends, family, and others who have asked questions about property investment.

What sets my book apart from other books on real estate investments is that I discuss the different types of properties I've had experience with and touch upon those experiences (both good and bad), my thoughts, and the important lessons, tips, and tricks I learnt along the way. While this book does use my experiences in the Australian market, I believe the logic, tools, and tactics I talk about are universal and can be applied anywhere.

2

Growing Up in the Australian Property Market

For a long as I can remember, I have heard about the great Australian dream of owning your own home, a place with a large backyard for kids to play in, where barbecues and summer parties will be had, and with a well-kept, impressive front yard that not only stands out but serves to tell all who pass by a little bit about the family who lives inside.

This has been the dream for many Australians, and in the past, you could be assured that if you worked hard and saved your money, one day you, too, would be able to own your slice of the dream, a shelter for all seasons, a place to start a family, build a life, and watch the world go by.

I remember the first house my parents had. It was a small eleven-square property in Gladstone Park. They built this house in the early 1970s. By today's standards, this property would be considered small for a home in the suburbs; however, at the time, it was an average-sized home and what my parents could afford. My parents lived within their means and worked hard to pay the mortgage off, while also trying to save for the future. They gradually paid down the mortgage, even with high interest rates. When their loan was paid off, they sold that little eleven-square property for more than four times its original value. This, combined with a new loan from the bank, was enough for them to build a twenty-four-square home in the Melbourne suburb of Greenvale.

In 1984, *Ghostbusters*, *Indiana Jones*, and *The Terminator* were in the cinemas. That was also the year we moved into the new house in Greenvale. Compared to our old home, this house seemed huge. It had the smell of a new house that was not quite finished. When we moved in, there were no curtains or carpets. Outside, instead of a garden, there was loose soil, and instead of a driveway, there was gravel from the curb to the front entry of the house. I have memories of my parents hanging bedsheets over the windows and setting up furniture; my bedroom had a concrete floor. Over time, the concrete was covered by carpet, curtains replaced bedsheets, fences marked the start and end of our property, and the soil gave way to a manicured garden.

I didn't know it yet, but my parents had just introduced me to the property market and gave me an insight to the thought processes of most Australians at that time. This was, buy what you could afford, repay what you could, and when you outgrew the property, sell it and buy a bigger one. When you think about it, it's a great way to stay in debt for longer (I will touch upon what I call good and bad debt later in this book).

I went to Good Shepherd Primary School, followed by high school at Salesian College Rupertswood—yes, the home of the Ashes, for those that like cricket. While at this agricultural school, I studied information technology, economics, and home economics. I thought these subjects would give me a good grounding and useful knowledge, which would help me after I left high school.

I found I enjoyed information technology, and my enjoyment was bolstered by having my own computer, which my parents bought for me one Christmas. Technology classes gave me an appreciation for creating things myself and working with materials such as metal, wood, and plastics. I learned many things I found useful in later life. Certainly, the training in information technology provided a career path that served me well. However, I was never taught about money and how to use it. Oh, my parents encouraged me to save and put my money into a piggy bank and then into a Dollarmites bank account, which was a special program by the Commonwealth Bank of Australia to encourage children to save money. When my savings accumulated, my parents taught me to take that money and put it into an interest-bearing account. I did this routinely.

After high school, I studied information technology at Tafe. After two years of study, the dean of the school observed a presentation that my team gave as part of our final exams. On the basis of our presentation, she asked me and two other team leaders for our résumés, which she sent to a company by the name of Bostik (yes, the Blu Tack people). I subsequently was called for an interview, which led to my first job in IT.

I was offered an entry-level position with an annual salary of twenty-three thousand dollars. By today's standards, that is half the current minimum wage. However, at that time, a three-bedroom house in Fawkner cost approximately seventy-two thousand dollars, and more importantly, you could get a beer on tap for around five dollars. I always had an interest in property; I enjoyed the idea of renovating places and loved watching shows like *Our House*, *Auction Squad*, and *Backyard Blitz*. They gave me ideas on how to go about renovating a house and garden. I also went to the annual Melbourne Home Show, which is hosted at the Melbourne Exhibition Centre. This event brings together manufacturers and construction companies to showcase their products and services.

I saved my money by putting half of my pay into a term deposit. It took some time, but after two years, I managed to save twenty thousand dollars—more than enough for a deposit on a property. So, like most people in their early twenties, I took this hard-earned money and did what you'd expect: I spent it on a car. It was a beautiful car, or so

I thought. It was a new Ford EF Falcon, lowered with a modified suspension, eighteen-inch wheel rims, two twelve-inch subwoofers, and an Alpine sound system. You get the idea! The value of that car today is probably eight hundred dollars, assuming it's still around. As for that house in Fawkner, it's worth over $730,000. Do I still kick myself about that decision? Yes, I certainly do. But it taught me a valuable lesson, not only about property but about money. Or should I say currency. I will talk about currency later in the book, but for now, the main thing to think about is the buying power my hard-earned savings achieved and the choices I made.

As time went on, my wages increased. I was quite fortunate to have a good manager, who took me under his wing, he helped increase my technical knowledge, and ensured that my salary kept pace with the market. By 2000, I was earning forty-three thousand dollars. This and some life changes like marriage meant that I finally needed to move out on my own. After looking at the many options, we decided upon purchasing land and building a house, as the homes we saw at the time, although pretty, didn't have everything we wanted. I also liked the idea of starting from scratch, like my parents did a decade or so earlier.

At the time, land in the up-and-coming suburb of Roxburgh Park was $65,000, and a four-bedroom Henley home was going for $114,000. When all was said and done, and with the addition of landscaping, tiles, and carpets, the house cost around $200,000. I have to say, though, that when we built our house, everything seemed to happen more rapidly than I remember it taking place for my parents. From start to finish, the process took around seven months. This was a contrast from when my parents built their second house. The house itself was built and ready for them to move in within ten months. However, it took them a good three years or so to complete everything to a similar point that we did in twelve months.

The house in Roxburgh Park served us well, and four years later, I had a new job and two young children. We decided to upscale and went from an 18-square home to a 40-square four-bedroom house in the suburb of Greenvale. Like with our first house, we decided to build. To cover the cost, we followed the same path that my parents did, which was to put the house in Roxburgh Park on the market. During the four years we had the property, its value had grown by approximately $25,000 a year; we finally sold it for $330,000. With these funds, we purchased the property in Greenvale by only increasing our loan by an extra $150,000.

Life went on, and our kids got bigger. We thought we had the Australian dream of a home in the suburbs, kids playing in the backyard, the whole nine yards, so to speak. The thing about dreams, though, is they can be hard to hold onto, and sometimes, what starts out as a dream can turn into a nightmare.

In 2009, everything changed. This was the year the global financial crisis (GFC) hit, and for the first time, I realised just how fragile the Australian dream could be. In June of that year, I had my first redundancy. One minute, I was employed, and the next minute, no job. I still remember the day it happened. My wife and children had gone overseas to visit family, and I stayed back, because I had work. I took a little time off before the family left to spend some time with them, as it would be a few months before I'd see them again. They departed on a Sunday afternoon. On the Monday morning, I was back to work. I came into the office and casually asked my boss if I had missed anything. I saw the colour drain from his face and he gave me a serious look. He called me into his office, asked me to shut the door, and had me take a seat. He then explained that things weren't going too well for the company; the GFC had hit the business hard. He went on to add that he had been asked to review the department's headcount and reduce costs as much as possible. What this meant was that after close to five years of service, my role was being made redundant.

However, he also mentioned that he pushed hard to get the maximum payout possible and would provide me with a reference or anything else that I needed. I thanked him for that and then went back to my desk to process what had happened. I think it was fair to say that I felt numb. It took a while for things to sink in. I looked around the office at my staff, just outside of the window, who used to report to me. For the first time, I was lost for words. Looking back at it, I think it was shock.

I felt the complete raft of emotions: anger, rage, helplessness, fear, all wrapped up in one moment. I felt embarrassed, as if I had done something wrong. Before this event, my career was on an upward trajectory. One job led to another job, which was slightly more senior than the previous role, in an industry which plays a pivotal role in an organisation. However, at the age of thirty-three, I found myself redundant, on the employment scrapheap, questioning my choices in a career, and for the first time uncertain about my future.

The drive home was a short one, but I was pretty much on autopilot all the way there. When I went inside, even though it was daytime, the house seemed dark. I was totally alone with my thoughts. To be redundant with a home loan, limited funds, no alternative means of income or assets to sell, in a time when the job market was hit hard. I thought to myself that this was not going to be easy, but it was a problem that had to be solved. I knew that there would be a significant amount of competition for what jobs remained.

For the first time, I took a hard look at my financial position. I had some funds as a result of my redundancy, but also a mortgage to pay and family to support. It was one of the most stressful times in my life and not something I would wish on anyone. For the first time, I found myself in an unemployment line to have my situation assessed to see what government services I could qualify for.

Even though I had lost my income stream and had minimal opportunity to find work, the government services officer said I did not qualify for immediate financial assistance, as I had funds in my account. They assigned me a case worker to help me find a job.

At the time, I felt this was a bit rough. Even though I had dutifully paid my taxes all my working career, it appeared that financial assistance would only present itself when things became dire and I was facing foreclosure. Yet by the same token, we have to pay into superannuation, so that when we retire, we aren't forced into a corner. I found these two things to be completely opposed to each other. I didn't care about having finances in my seventies. I cared about being able to make it through this situation without having to sell everything I had worked so hard to build over my career.

Six weeks after my redundancy, and by a stroke of luck, I managed to find a contract role at a telecommunications company. This position started immediately and also paid more than my previous job. I have to admit, it gave me great satisfaction to tell my government assigned caseworker that I had to decline a position they found for me, as I had a job paying close to three times what their opportunity offered. But I was still thinking about my finances and how close I had come.

I had been so focused on my career, doing a good job, building relationships, and climbing the work ladder, I didn't think about what I was doing with the money I earned, other than using it to pay off the loan for our property, as well as living expenses.

After how close we came to losing everything, my focus shifted. Whilst I realised the importance of being able to generate income through work, I also saw how critical it was to understand what was happening with the cash flow coming in. I always maintained a budget on a spreadsheet that tracked my loan structure and expenditures. I expanded this spreadsheet to include all my spending, which helped to build up my financial reserves. But that wasn't enough. My thoughts were, if it was possible to become redundant once, it was possible to become redundant again, and as I became older, it may become harder to secure work. So as my savings grew, I also started to look at options and research how I could create additional income streams. The first thing that caught my eye was the book *Rich Dad, Poor Dad*. I found this book hard to put down, and it certainly changed the way I looked at my assets and liabilities, as well as my income. I then started to look into books by Steve McKnight, specifically *From 0 to 130 Properties in 3.5 Years*. I talked to whoever I could find who had an investment property.

3

New, Off-the-Plan Build

When I finally saved enough for a deposit, I spoke to an accountant; I was nervous about purchasing a property. What if I couldn't make the repayments? What if the property didn't rent? What if the value of the property went down? What if there were issues with the property? What if I missed something? You get the idea. Even though I took every precaution and filled my head with as much information as possible, I still felt fear about investing my savings into property. I remember talking to my uncle and aunty, who had an investment property. After telling them what I was thinking about doing and sharing some of my concerns, I found my aunt's response quite simple and funny.

She said, "If you can't afford it, sell it."

Such a matter-of-fact response, but yet so true. Ultimately, I was purchasing an asset. The asset had value, and if I couldn't afford it, I could simply sell the thing. I had researched all the information I could, talked to everyone I could think about who knew something about property, yet I was still nervous.

At that point, a little voice spoke in my head. It said, "Shut up and do it."

So with that in mind, I got to work and began to search real estate websites, looking for a property that met my requirements. After some work, I found one I liked which was in my price range.

I bought my first investment property in October 2010. It was a four-bedroom townhouse, off the plan in Melton, West Victoria. I paid $265,000 for the property, and I still own it. In today's economy, it's worth double the purchase price. After I bought it, I spent a complete year monitoring it. The property rented quite quickly, and for the next year, I watched it closely and made sure I understood everything about how the investment worked.

I learnt many things about property investment from this property, like making sure your figures are accurate and having a tolerance for changes. For example, interest rates do change; they can go up or down. So factoring in some tolerance to cope with increases is prudent. Setting some funds aside for issues that might crop up is also a good thing. With new places, repairs aren't much of an issue, and when something does break, it may still be under warranty.

But people do leave, and there are costs associated with this. It's prudent to set some money aside for advertising, garden maintenance, and loan payments for when the property isn't rented. What worked for me was to use an offset account on my investment loan, as a place to park funds for this. The advantage was, while the funds sat, they actually worked against the interest on the loan, and they were in a location that was easy to access, but kept separate from my everyday spending, so I wasn't tempted to spend it. This does fly in the face of negative gearing, which I will talk about later in the book, but it worked for me.

I also learnt to get a depreciation schedule done as soon as I purchased the property. A number of companies out there can do a depreciation schedule. Essentially, this is a report that considers all the components of the house that wear down over time. These items are different for every house, but when it's provided to your accountant, they can determine what you can claim back on depreciation.

The last thing this property taught me was how to claim expenses. I purchased the house with the intent of it being a negative geared property. My research at that point was that this was the done thing with property investment. As I paid taxes, negative gearing was an allowed deduction that would allow me to recoup some of my taxable income. Some would say this is how rich people get around paying taxes. I have always had an issue with that notion. The way I looked at it, with the exception of some, if you were indeed rich, then you wouldn't need to invest in the first place. In my experience, the people who invest in properties and utilise negative gearing have worked hard and gotten to a point in life where they can pay all their living expenses and have some residual money left over each month. Instead of spending this money, they invest it, so they can have a brighter future, a bit more certainty and less stress, should something happen or should their circumstances change.

If negative gearing did not exist, it would reduce the attraction for some people to invest in the property market. As our population is growing, this means that demand would outstrip supply. This creates a couple of issues; firstly, the properties that currently exist would become more valuable, as there are fewer of them. Whilst this is good for those who have already purchased a property, for those wishing to buy their first home, this only serves to move the target more quickly. In addition, the shortage in properties would also mean that the rental market prices would also increase; this forces out some of the lower income earners into lower grade properties (or worse).

As a result, the government would need to step in and create affordable housing. This is not a theoretical model; this actually occurred in the past. If you look at the Melbourne skyline, it has a number of old commission buildings, and there are a number of ex commission homes in the suburbs of Geelong and Broadmeadows. This all sounds quite nice, in a socialist way. However, when you consider the amount of resources in terms of taxes that would need to be diverted to create these properties, and ensuing their upkeep, the current solution seems most efficient: encouraging people to invest, which also puts less strain on the economy, which has enough to deal with.

2010.08.07

2010.08.07

16

2010.08.07

4

Old Properties

After waiting a full year to learn how a rental property operated and calculate what expenses I'd incur, I decided to try again. But this time, I didn't go for a new property, nor did I go for a small apartment. I bought an old three-bedroom house in the suburb of Norlane. After an exhaustive search, I found a small timber weatherboard property on a large flat block. The house was built in the early 1940s and was tired. Due to its age, there were no warranties. So I had an independent building inspection carried out to assess if the property was structurally sound. The report came back quite favourably, despite the age, and so I started negotiations with the agent. After some back and forth, I purchased the house for $185,000. Unlike the Melton property, this one needed work.

I got the keys to the property on a Saturday morning; I stepped inside, and with all the furniture gone, the property seemed smaller. I was greeted with a combination of a musty smell mixed with old tobacco. The walls and ceiling were at one time white, but over time, they had that yellow tinge from people smoking inside. The carpets were worn, a combination of a pastel pink in one bedroom, brown in the others, and what looked like an old Axminster carpet in the hallway and living room. Interestingly enough, the Axminster was the exact same pattern that my grandmother had in her house, which I remember crawling on as a child. I was tempted to keep the carpet in the living room and hallway for sentimental sake. But it was an investment, not something to be sentimental about. Also, with the amount of work it would have taken to get the smell out of the carpet, it was much easier to change it.

As for the windows, most of them were covered with old torn lace and those metal blinds that were so popular in the 1970s and really great to get a paper cut on, if you were unlucky enough to run your finger along the edge of it. The kitchen was small and L-shaped, and it was probably last upgraded in the 1960s, and as for the bathroom, well, this was the one area which wasn't too bad, as it seemed to have had a 1990s update.

The outside of the house was painted in a Kermit the Frog green. The front of the property had an old hedge which had been lovingly manicured and looked at least forty years old, the fences were timber, and the backyard had a large metal garage/workshop. Like most houses, the Hills Hoist was right in the centre of the backyard. A large lemon tree was down the back, and behind the garage was what looked like a veggie patch that had long since been left to the weeds.

I remember thinking there was so much work to do on this property to get it ready to rent. But I couldn't have been happier. Up until that point, I had done handyman jobs for others, but the properties I owned were all new and didn't really need any work. I was on a deadline, though, as time was money, and the longer that property was not rented, the more it cost me.

Fortunately, I had some friends and family who were happy to pitch in and help me. This helped make things go quickly, and having some project management skills was also beneficial, with things like ordering bins for the rubbish; selecting paint colours; and having rollers, brushes, and tools ready had all been considered and sorted before I took possession of the property.

The look on the selling agent's face was funny. He gave me the keys in the morning but popped around to see how I was getting along later on. By the time he arrived, the carpets were stripped out, and an undercoat had gone onto trims, doors, ceilings, and walls. The garden was getting some attention, and the kitchen tiles were getting a light sand in preparation for painting. I believe the words out of his mouth were "Holy f---," followed by, "you weren't kidding when you said you're going to do a commando reno on the property."

We worked a full day that Saturday and finished around one o'clock in the morning. Sunday morning, we started a bit later, around eleven, but also worked back till around midnight. But by Monday, pretty much everything was finished, with the exception of new carpets, which were completed by Wednesday. By the end of the week, the leasing agent was taking photos of the property in preparation to have it leased. The property raised quite a bit of interest, and within three weeks, we had several tenant applications to choose from.

So why did I buy this property? What was it that pushed me in the direction of purchasing a house like this? Well, when I was thinking about purchasing a new property, I started shopping around for someone who could do a depreciation schedule. During this process, I reflected on the depreciation schedule and what it is. Essentially, it allows you to expense the components of the property that wear down over time. I pondered this and wondered why, if parts of the property wear out over time, its value goes up over time? After all, if I purchased a new car, after ten years, even if it was a luxury car, I wouldn't expect it to be worth more. I would expect it to be worth significantly less. So what is it about a property that increases its value? The only thing I could think of was the land.

Certainly, this was validated by some of the books I was reading at the time. In essence, what it came down to was, as the demand for housing increases, new suburbs are created farther out from towns, cities, and major hubs. In so doing, the land closer to where people want to live and work becomes more desirable. Now, whilst most of these locations have tiny houses, lacking in amenities, more often than not, the block they are on can accommodate a significant amount of units. These properties then become more valuable, as they become prime properties for redevelopment, be it by subdivision, demolition, new build, or renovation. This was the key motivation for me purchasing the property in Norlane.

The other thing I should mention here is to always check the fine print. The key things I thought about when I was shopping for a property that could be redeveloped later on, was to confirm the rules. Certain suburbs in Victoria have caveats on the land, restricting the subdivision of the properties that are under a certain size. As a general rule, if you are under 600 metres square, you will need to build a case to subdivide.

The other factor was easements and anything that ran under the ground which could impact future development. This is where Section 32 / contract or sale came in handy and also a service called Dial Before you

Dig. With the land checked and confirmed to be clear of easements or anything that could impact upon a future build, I moved forward and purchased the property.

Once again, as soon as this property was leased and had a tenant in it, I started to track its progress; I recorded all the expenses the property had so that when it came to tax time, I would get the best return possible. As with the Melton property, this one was a negatively geared property; it cost more than it made, but the value of the property was going up, and the loss could be deducted, which improved my tax liability, so I was quite happy with it.

I was now at a point where I had two investment properties in addition to our residence. These financial commitments took some work to balance. But I remembered my aunty's words: "If you can't manage it, sell it." These properties, though, did give me some comfort that should something happen to my income stream in the future, I could simply sell a property and use the proceeds of the sale to ensure that my lifestyle could continue without an issue. This was especially comforting to me, as my children were quite young, and being able to provide a stable education was important to me.

Years earlier, I spoke to the same uncle and aunty about education and what they did with their kids. Their point of view about education was interesting. When it came to primary school, they favoured location over most other things and suggested that for primary school, most schools are fine. Going into secondary school, though, they recommended doing research to understand what services a school offered, what their pass rates were, and what percentage of students went on from that school into university. They also suggested I consider private schools as an option and get on their waiting list as early as possible.

Soon after my first child was born, I started to research all the schools in my area. All of them, even the government schools, seemed pretty good. It came down to what I could afford and also the varied courses and facilities being offered. For my education, I went to a Catholic primary school and then a private school for secondary. The secondary school that I went to was Salesian College Rupertswood. At the time, it was not a coed school, but it had an extensive selection of rural, economic, and technical courses I found interesting. Certainly the technical courses in wood, metal work, and electronics, whilst they had no bearing in the career path I selected, provided me with skills that proved quite valuable in later life. With this in mind, I started looking at schools.

We had a number of schools in our area, all of which had pros and cons. I analysed both public and private, reviewed their respective pass rates over a ten-year period, as well as the percentage of students that went on to university. I was leaning towards a private school, but getting on a waiting list required an enrolment fee of fifteen hundred dollars. At the time, that was a sizable amount, which made me wonder. If the enrolment fee took some struggle to come up with, could I manage the annual tuition fees?

I thought about this for some time, and then once again, that voice in the back of my head spoke up and said, "Shut up and do it. You have ten years to build up finances and work it out."

I enrolled my oldest child onto the waiting list for Aitken College. Aside from being close to where we lived, it also was set out on a large parcel of land and offered an extensive number of subjects. So my wife and I were quite happy with our decision, as we felt that we had done all we could to ensure our child would have the best education we could afford.

I now was more motivated than ever to invest further in the property market. I considered my situation; I had been working for a few years but had quite some time yet left in my career. This meant I had the time to allow my investments to grow. So for the next investment, I decided to do something different again and looked farther out, much, much, much farther out. This time, I went rural and started looking at some suburbs that were three or more hours from Melbourne.

5

Rural Properties

I used Google Maps to have a look at rural towns in Victoria. Once I had a list of towns, I researched them to learn more about the population. To my surprise, I found that some of these towns weren't that small, and some had a population that was consistently growing, year on year. This was good, as I didn't want to invest in a location which had no need for a rental property. Once I knew which towns to target, I then used my trusty property search sites to look for properties in these country towns. Whilst I knew that the prices would be lower than in Melbourne, I was still very much surprised when I found you could actually buy a property of considerable size for a fraction of the cost of what you could get in Melbourne. I thought there had to be a catch to this. Whilst land value does play a factor, the prices I saw were, well, ridiculous. For instance, I bought a small three-bedroom property in Geelong for $185,000. This property rented for $210 a week. In Horsham, I could buy the same size house on a similar size block for $80,000, which would rent between $175 to $220 a week. So to summarise, I could spend less than half the amount I would for a property in Geelong and get a similar amount of money in rent. Like I said, ridiculous.

I needed to know more about Horsham. It seemed too good to be true and risky. After doing some research on the suburb, I learned that it was a key location in the region and served as a central point for farming in the area. The town itself wasn't small, with a population of around nineteen thousand people. The next step was to go and have a look for myself. So one morning, my wife and I took a drive from Melbourne to Horsham. Three and a half hours later and halfway to Adelaide, we came to the town of Horsham.

We took a few laps around town to get an understanding of what the facilities were like. I thought the town was quite pretty and easy to drive through, with a very green park close to the centre of town and clean streets. It seemed to have everything: schools, grocery shops, fast food places, restaurants, and pubs. There is also a nice river that runs close by the town centre. We went for lunch at the White Hart Hotel, a local pub. This was a good chance to have a look around. During lunch, we saw a flood of tradespeople coming and going. This was a good sign, as tradespeople meant that the town had development going on. Development meant that the town was building and not contracting and going into a decline.

One of my greatest fears was investing in a location that had no rental market. I did my homework on this town before we made the trip out. It had a vacancy rate of 1%. By comparison, the vacancy rate in Melbourne was around 4.7%. So to summarise, in this town the purchase price for properties was low. The rental return was high, and the vacancy rates were low. These facts show why this town was of interest to me. It certainly was ticking all of my boxes in terms of risk.

After we finished lunch, we went to see a couple of properties I found on the internet in the area. I set a budget of $100k for a house, with a return of $160 as a minimum rental target. We looked at these properties, and now that we had an understanding of the location, we were in a better position to make an informed decision.

Three properties seemed to fit my criteria. One was a two-bedroom timber weatherboard on the outskirts of town, which was rented out.

It had a large backyard, no garage, but some large sheds at the back of the property. Inside, it looked a bit tired. The walls were what I call a smoker's yellow from years of people smoking inside the house. The floors were dirty and had worn carpet in all rooms, except the kitchen, where it had old lino. There was also the faint smell of dog. The little voice in my head said one word: "Next."

The next house, a three-bedroom property, was a bit cleaner. It had a single-car carport, attached to the side of the house. The house itself was painted a bright yellow and had a ramp for disabled access that led to a porch. Inside, the house seemed old but had recently been painted. It seemed to have been painted in a rush, as there was some paint spray on the floors, which were unpolished timber boards. The kitchen was old but in good shape and still quite functional.

This particular property was in between tenants, but I was told that the house had been rented for $150 for a number of years. The former tenant was an older gentlemen who left to go into a nursing home about a month earlier. The agent went on to say that the seller had since cleaned up the property and carried out some minor renovation works after the tenant vacated. She estimated that the property could be rented for about $180 a week. This certainly seemed like a good deal, but I did have one other property to look at, so we thanked the agent for showing us the property and said we'd let her know.

Property number 3 was the closest to the town centre. This one was still rented. Another agent met us at the property to take us through it. It was a green three-bedroom home. As we walked up to the property, I could see that the porch was not exactly level, but still quite functional. When we walked inside, it had the faint smell of dog. I was then greeted by a large but very obedient and docile German shepherd that came to be patted and then went back into the living room to curl up next to the wood fire heater. The walls were a two tone with a brownish pink, with a picture rail, and then white for the remainder of the wall. The ceiling was white. The house was around 10 to 12 squares. The kitchen was small but functional, and the laundry was on the outside of the house. It was not as bad as the first property we had looked at, but not as clean as the second one.

The backyard had an unusual shed. It was roughly 3.5 metres high 8 metres long and about 8 metres wide, and there was a carport attached to it, which was half the size of the shed again. The shed was extremely well built and had three-phase power installed. The agent explained that the previous owner was a mechanic and ran his business from that shed. It occurred to me that the cost of the shed alone would be close to the asking price of the property. I also noticed that the property behind this one had been torn down, and in its place, three units were being built.

So now I had a decision to make: Property 1, 2, or 3? The first property was easily discounted; however, 2 and 3 were both similarly priced. Property 2 was cleaner and could potentially rent for more than Property 3, which was leased at that time. But with Property 3, even though it was returning less, it seemed to be a higher value property overall, which would mean that in the unlikely event of the tenants exiting it would only take another one of those commando-type clean-ups, and the property could then go quickly back onto the market, where it would rent out for the same if not more.

This time, the voice in my head was quicker in its estimation, and I heard those words again: "Shut up and do it." So I put in an offer for Property 3 and, after a bit of negotiation, purchased it for $97,000. I remember telling some of my friends about this purchase and seeing the look of utter disbelief on their faces after I told them how much it was renting for, how big the property was, and how little I had paid.

Just after this purchase, I changed roles at my workplace and found myself in a more senior position, with increased cash flow. Whilst some people would have celebrated and seen this as an opportunity to upgrade items in the house or book a holiday, I saw this as an opportunity to increase my investment portfolio. After a short probationary period, I contacted my bank and enquired about my borrowing capacity. It seemed that whilst I had purchased a couple of properties, the combination of the increase in pay and the addition of the Horsham property, which actually made more money than it cost to run, resulted in my additional borrowing capacity being close to $400,000.

I thought about the property in Norlane. I originally bought out there because of the generous land size. Other things influenced my decision to buy out there; Norlane had so much going for it. It was close to the water, it had a large population, there was a diverse amount of industry and business in the area, and there was a railway line that went directly to Melbourne. I remember thinking to myself that places such Williamstown and Altona once started out like that. What made me return, though, was reading up on a project called New Norlane that was announced in 2012. This project was to deliver 342 new homes onto 200 vacant blocks of land on a budget of $80 million. My thoughts about this were, 200 blocks of land but almost double the amount of houses being built could only be achieved with subdivision of the existing blocks. This then would mean that the value of land could increase.

Once again, I used realestate.com.au and domain.com.au to research the area and sorted them on land size and cheapest property. A number of properties came up in my search, but one of them stood out of the crowd. It was an old weatherboard, deceased estate on a corner block. I spoke to the agent and arranged to see the property on a Saturday afternoon. I decided to make a day of it and took my family out to Geelong; however, I neglected to say that I was considering buying another property.

We spent much of the day on the Geelong Esplanade. There was a festival on, and the kids spent much of the time running around on the sand, going on some of the rides, and rolling down a steep hill next to the boardwalk. After a fish and chip lunch, I said we were going to take a quick drive and check something out. So we got into the car and drove the ten minutes to Norlane. We pulled up to the property, where I was greeted by the agent. My wife gave me a funny look, and we all proceeded to go inside the house.

It wasn't the oldest property in Norlane, but certainly had been there for some time. The windows had been replaced some time in the late 1970s, the walls were covered in pink wallpaper, the carpets were clean but worn, and the kitchen was a mess and beyond saving. Knowing that the property owner was deceased, and having the confidence in my finances sorted, I made an offer that was $25k below the asking price. To sweeten the deal, I told the agent I'd remove the subject-to-finance clause and wave the cooling-off period. With that, we left the property and went back to the esplanade to enjoy the rest of the day.

On the way back, I remember my wife giving me the "WTF" look and saying I bought property like most people buy milk. I found that comment funny. Whilst on the surface, it may have seemed that I was quite blasé about the whole transaction, I really wasn't. I had done my homework; I was confident in the area and was taking a chance on buying something I believed was undervalued. The only thing that concerned me was the kitchen; how much would it cost to change it, should I actually get the property?

Around 2 p.m., I received a call from the agent. He had two words for me: "Offer accepted." I thanked him for his work and asked him to email me the details, and we'd get it sorted during the week.

The terms of settlement were sixty days; later, at a family event, I told my cousin I had bought another property. I mentioned the particulars of the property and said I was renovating the kitchen. He said his dad was renovating a kitchen at their beach house in Phillip Island, and they were going to dump the old kitchen.

The first words out of my mouth were "Can I have it?" I should note that my cousin's parents were the same uncle and aunty who gave me the advice about rental properties in the first place. I spoke to them about the kitchen, and they were more than happy to give me the old one. I just needed to pick it up, which meant a trip out to Phillip Island.

I hired a canopy trailer, and my cousin and I picked up the kitchen and brought it home. Whilst the kitchen was a freebie, it needed a bit of modification, as it needed to be an L shape, and what I had was a U-shaped kitchen. So whilst I was waiting for settlement, I went to work on the kitchen pieces. This is where some of my high school woodworking skills, as well as having a two-car garage, came in handy. I began modifying the kitchen cabinets and bought paint and other materials required to get the new property ready for renting.

The day after settlement, I picked up the keys to the property and went into a demo mode. The kitchen was the first to go, followed by carpets. Next was the wallpaper. I have nothing against wallpaper, but it's one of those things that can hide serious cracks and structural issues that need to be attended to. And this paper was definitely out of style and had a musky smell after being on the walls for decades.

What I learnt with this property about renovating was priceless. The first thing is, wherever possible, go for industrial equipment. I initially tried to remove the wallpaper by spraying a solution onto the wallpaper that eats into the glue and allows the paper to be removed with a scraper. In theory, great, and it worked fine for some of the rooms. But in a few of the rooms, the paper just stuck to the wall so hard that I ended up hiring a wallpaper steamer. That made light work of the walls and allowed the paper to be removed quickly and easily.

The other thing I learnt was, no floor is even. The demolition of the kitchen took a few hours to do. However, the installation of the new one took all day. The hardest part was making sure the base was absolutely flat. This took quite some time to perfect. It might sound a bit pedantic to make sure the kitchen cupboards were absolutely level. However, if it's not, things could roll off the bench tops, and doors often open by themselves; also, water doesn't drain property from sinks, and tiles don't quite line up properly.

Unlike the first property I renovated, which took under a week to completely renovate and get back onto the rental market, this house took significantly longer. From start to finish, it took approximately three weeks, after which the property was handed over to a leasing agent, who had it rented about a month later.

In 2013, I had investments in Melton, Geelong, and Horsham. The company I was working for was undergoing a transformation and streamlining its processes. The translation to this was staff shedding. I got wind there were redundancies coming. It had been four years since my first redundancy. This time, though, things were different. I had built up a significant amount of resources, it wasn't a GFC period, and I was in an industry that was in demand. I considered the idea of volunteering for a redundancy. This then would allow me to test the structures I had been building over the past four years, whilst at the same time getting a payout. From a logical perspective, this made sense; however, the notion of offering to be made redundant made me nervous.

Then that little voice, which had been quiet for some time, piped up and said, "Shut up and do it." So with that in mind, I went into HR and informed them that I would be OK with a voluntary redundancy. They agreed to consider my request, and two weeks later, the organisation approved it.

Once free of my job, I contacted my bank and gave instructions for all my loans to go to interest only. This was part of my plan. Whilst I was working, I put each of my properties on a principal-and-interest repayment structure, which reduced the loan amount and over time would allow the property to be completely paid off. However, now that I wasn't employed, my idea was to make reduced payments, which would allow the properties to effectively sit, and the funds that would have been put towards the loan would then be utilised to support me, whilst I looked for a new role. In theory, this would allow me to retain the property assets, without reducing my saving.

Once I set this structure in motion, I then monitored it, and it seemed to work brilliantly. The rents coming in were sufficient to keep the interest-only repayments on the investment property loans, but created just enough residual cash to pay the interest-only component of the home loan for the property I lived in and limited funds to ensure that all the normal bills associated with living were paid for as well. This was actually gratifying to watch, or at least I thought so. I had successfully managed to come up with a structure that in times of need, where my income stopped, gave me an option to hold us in a kind of limbo, until I started working again.

After four months or so, I once again found employment. However, the interest-only option had to continue for a set period. At the time, I thought I could simply make extra repayments into my redraw account so that when the period finished, I could make a bulk repayment and move back to principal-and-interest payments.

I learned that you have to be very careful when entering an interest-only loan. It is important to know if the loan term will be increased or not. I was on a thirty-year loan cycle, and the bank did have an option that could be exercised to go onto interest-only for up to five years in the event of job loss or some other hardship. This is what I exercised during the redundancy period. However, this option did not increase the loan duration. So what happened was that after the one-year interest-only period finished, the loan reverted to a principal-and-interest loan. The repayments increased to compensate and ensure that we would hit the target of the loan finishing in the thirty-year period.

Whilst this was good, I felt that I had wasted time. The reason for this was that whilst the property's value would have gone up over the period, I wasn't getting the maximum value out of the money I had parked into the offset account. There was a clause in the loan where if it went from a principal-and-interest loan into an interest-only loan, the offset would also change. It went from 100 per cent offset to somewhere around 10 per cent. This meant that 90 per cent of the value of the funds parked into this account just sat there and did not reduce the loan amount.

6

Principal-and-Interest versus Interest-Only Loans

This is an interesting topic for investors. With all my home loans and investment loans, I have always gone for a principal-and-interest loan. This is a conflict if you use negative gearing, which allows you to claim the loss you incur from an investment property against your taxable income. Hence, if you are using a principal-and-interest loan, over time as the amount on the loan reduces, so too does the interest being charged for the loan. This then also reduces the value you can claim back on tax. With an interest-only loan, you only pay the interest incurred; the loan itself is not paid down.

The theory behind interest-only is that you pay the interest and then claim a deduction when you do your tax return. This deduction will remain largely the same and only fluctuates when interest rates move up or down. The property, however, should increase in value. The increase or capital gains can either be realised by selling the property or used as equity to purchase another investment property.

Either of these options can be utilised to build wealth. Investors must decide which option to make for themselves, based on their personal situation and what they want to achieve.

I have always opted for a principal-and-interest loan, as I like the idea of being able to hold onto the property over the long term and only selling if it makes sense to do so and, more importantly, selling on my terms.

In my circumstances, I am concerned about "what if?" questions: What if I can't work? What if the rules around interest-only loans change? What if the property itself goes down in value, or what if all three of these things occur? The smaller the debt, at any given time, would mean that I have more options. Furthermore, I see property investments as a way to create wealth but also as a life raft, should something financially bad happen to me. These life rafts can be sacrificed to protect what's most important to me. This is why, as soon as the interest-only period ended, I went back to principal-and-interest loans.

The other thing is, banks only allow you to run interest-only loans for a short period of time (five years seems to be the limit). At that point, an investor then refinances to another institution and continues on. It is possible to run this type of option for as long as you are employed. But what happens when you retire? At that point, you don't have an income to support the refinance option, nor do you have an income to make negative gearing attractive. So what happens at this point is, people who utilised this option tend to sell the property. They typically sell it for much more than the purchase price, which would then cover the payout of the loan as well as any capital gains tax, hopefully leaving them with surplus funds they can use to support their new lifestyle.

7

Apartments

I knew someone who was looking to invest in a property. They owned their own home but wanted a nest egg. They knew I was into property investment and sought out my advice, just as I did years earlier. I explained to them that not all properties are the same. They are unique, and each gets a different result.

However, you need to select the property that works best with what you want to do. I mentioned the properties I had bought in Horsham, Geelong, and Melton. As you know, I watch each of my properties extremely closely. In addition, after asking for my borrowing capacity, the bank conducted an evaluation of my assets. The result of the evaluation gave me an approximate current value for each property. Over the past twelve months, the Melton property, an off-the-plan townhouse, had increased in value by approximately $25k. The Horsham property, which was tired but still functional, increased by $10k, and the Geelong property increased by close to $65k. I knew exactly why the Geelong property had the highest growth. It wasn't luck; the value of the land had increased, as a result of the New Norlane project.

So my feedback to them was to consider what they wanted the property to do. For instance, were they looking for a nest egg so they could live off the rental return, or were they looking for a property they could use to negative gear and sell for more at a later stage?

They were not sure about those questions but said they wanted to improve their position and have more assets, so when they got older, they wouldn't have to rely on pensions, which they thought might not exist in the future, or handouts from friends or family. I agreed that pensions may not exist into the future, as the services being asked from the government were being pushed, and at some point, cuts may be the only option to ensure that basic services operate. This notion seems to drive most people to invest in property. This is not because they are rich, but more because they are uncertain about the future and want to have a sense of control over it.

They purchased a property in Prahran. It was a two-bedroom off-the-plan apartment, in an area that was built up. Whilst I would agree location is a key item, I was a little concerned with this one. I knew there was quite a bit of construction already in that area and wondered if this would result in an oversupply. If so, the knock-on effect would be that rental prices could drop, as tenants would have greater choice and so could negotiate a better deal. As the apartment was brand new, there was nothing that could be done to add more value to it. So logically, this meant that in the short term, it could actually go down in value.

I ran into them a few years later and asked how they went with that apartment. By the looks on their faces, it didn't look good. They purchased the apartment for around $570,000, and for the first year, everything was great. In fact, better than great, as the developer found a tenant and guaranteed the first year's lease to ensure they had an stress-free transition into being a property investor.

However, when the rental contract finished, the tenant decided to not renew the lease, and that's when the trouble started. They had problems finding a tenant willing to pay what the previous tenant paid. The real-estate agent suggested lowering the rent, and they did; about six weeks later, they had a new tenant. However, the reduction in rent meant they had to come up with the rest of the money to pay the mortgage.

They also found that when the property was revalued, it came in at $150,000 less than they paid for it. On top of that, some maintenance items required work, increasing their costs further. The experience left them with a sour taste for property investment; two years after they bought this property, they sold it for less than they paid and vowed to never invest in real estate again.

Looking at this critically, it wasn't because it was an apartment that resulted in this outcome. This seemed to be purely a case of demand and supply, or in this case oversupply into the market. The result of the oversupply meant that tenants had greater choice. This drove rents down and also affected the resale of the property, as investors could purchase new properties at a similar price point. Therefore, those who wanted to sell their apartment had to make the property attractive to a prospective purchaser, which thereby drove the prices down.

Would this last forever? No, typically, time is what is required. Time for the developments in the area to complete, time for the population to increase, and time for the supply of new properties to be consumed. Typically, once the supply is exhausted, rental prices tend to rise, as there are fewer choices for renters. This then makes the properties more attractive to investors, who start to buy them, driving prices up. There are a few more variables to this equation. For instance, industry and facilities also play a factor. Desirable features such as schools, universities, shops, and access to beaches and restaurants tend to attract people wanting to live in these locations quicker than places which lack these facilities.

8

Money Is Not a Dirty Word

I purchased properties in suburbs that had certain characteristics. They were locations I believed were undervalued, where the population was not in a decline, and where the vacancy rate was low. I had properties in Geelong, Melton, and Horsham. At this point, I considered myself a fairly seasoned investor, but like with anything, the more you learn, the more you realise how little you know. I always enjoyed reading books on property investing and attended at least one seminar a year to see what I could learn.

In these books and seminars, one of the key takeaways I found valuable is hearing about what others have done. The sharing of experiences of what people have done and the results, both good and bad, were enormously helpful. Many seminars mention that financial skills are not taught in schools. I certainly never learned about compound interest, currency, budgeting, or my favourite: the pros and cons of a credit card. After people graduate from high school and start working, they don't know what to do.

Here's a good example: I knew a woman who was educated and could do financial gymnastics with the funds she had available to her. She worked for years as a financial planner and in a superannuation fund providing advice. But when she left school, she started working and found she was eligible for a credit card. She immediately signed up for a card, with no concept about the repayment structure and interest rates. She believed it to be, as she put it, "free money," and hence did what most teens would have done: retail therapy. Moreover, when the debts started to add up and needed to be paid, she would sign up for another card and use that to pay off the old card. She has since learnt some very hard lessons, which could have been avoided if someone gave her the information she needed to make an informed decision.

Even in my own family, my mother doesn't like it when I mention what I do or the properties I have. I'm not sure if this is a generational thing, but it seems to be imbedded into us to not discuss finances; those who do are considered boastful and rude. To some of my family, it's perceived as showing off to talk about your assets. However, if you mentioned that you lost weight or went on a special diet, you'd be congratulated, given a high five, and encouraged to keep it up.

I'm not saying that when you meet someone, you should talk about your finances, and if I am at a casual event, I don't go out of my way to tell someone what I have. But if someone shows an interest and asks about my investments, I share the information, including the good, the bad and the lessons I learned.

In contrast, with close friends, especially those who invest in property, I enjoy talking about what we are doing and learning about what others are doing. Certainly, I have learnt a substantial amount about what to do and not to do from listening to my friends who invest; we discuss agent rates, tradespeople, commercial and residential investments, and even investing in small businesses.

A lot of material has been written about investment. This book is yet another example, and there are so many books, seminars, and people who are ready to show you how to generate wealth in a multitude of ways. All of them started in a similar way: learning, developing, sometimes failing, but ultimately using what they learnt to do better. The information and insight they learnt is valuable. But so too are the stories and lessons learnt from the people around you. For example, my family came from India. Several ancestors created wealth through owning property and small businesses, but in only one or two generations, that wealth was split up and wasted away to nothing. In previous generations, family members owned farmland which today is part of a major city; gold sovereigns, property and a large taxi service in Pakistan. All of this disappeared without a trace.

Compared to the rest of the world, Australia is a young country, but we do have our share of famous families who worked hard and generated significant wealth. The rest of the world has families such as the Rothschilds, Carnegies, and Astors, to name a few. If you research these families, you find they all started from humble beginnings, with the same stresses, concerns, and drive that we all have. However, as a result of creative thinking, good timing, and or the ability to take advantage of an opportunity, they managed to create an immense amount of wealth. They do deserve credit for this. But when you look at what happened to some of these families over time, the wealth accrued over time degrades, as a result of being diluted through more descendants or due to economic changes. On a smaller scale, the issue is similar in my own family. I understand how the passage of time can erode wealth. It certainly does seem that even when you are successful, there are forces working against you to reduce your income and savings.

However, one family seems to stand out for creating a significant amount of wealth; more importantly, they managed to maintain their wealth over the generations. That family is the Rockefellas. Over the years, a number of articles described how this family preserves its wealth. It revolves around sharing information about what their money is doing and how its being used. In addition, there is focus put on preserving the history of the family and sharing that knowledge. Family members learn about their ancestors but more importantly understand why they made the decisions they made, what happened as a result, and also the struggles they went through, which ultimately benefited the current generation.

9

Why Do People Invest?

I've often wondered what makes someone invest in property. There are so many books on the subject (including this one). I find it interesting to talk to other investors and read books by people who have gone through their own journey. It struck me that they seemed so confident in what they were doing, and they appeared proud of the choices they made and the struggles they went through to create these opportunities. Oddly enough, I've never heard about anyone being nervous or having reservations about this type of investment.

I came from a mixed family background. Some family members are open to the idea of property investment, but others would never consider this type of investment. My parents fell into the second category. I guess you could say they are risk-averse. There is nothing wrong with this, and it's quite understandable. They immigrated to Australia in the late 1960s. When they arrived, they had a few suitcases containing clothes and personal effects, but not much else. They worked hard, and my mum studied hard, to improve and climb the work ladder. As for dad he did long hours as a shift worker. There primary source of income was what they earned working. In fact, the only investment they dabbled in was investing in their super.

This was the type of financial grounding and education I had growing up: study hard, get a job, use your career to generate an income, save your money, and once you had enough, buy what you wanted. And only take a loan when it's absolutely necessary. I was also taught to pay the loan off before moving onto something else or taking out another loan. If I wanted to increase my income, I needed to demonstrate my value at work, and if I did a good job, I would be rewarded with an increase in income. I soon learnt about other options, which challenged these foundational lessons I had been taught. My parents' way of doing things seemed to be a slow-and-steady approach, an approach that was tried and tested. It reminded me of the Tortoise and the Hare fable most children learn about, where the slow and consistent Tortoise won his race against the Hare.

This education led me to take a risk-averse approach to property investment and spend a substantial amount of time asking "What if?" questions. That was important, as whilst most people talk about how good it is to invest, there is always a risk. It is not a certainty that every investment in property works. However, I was driven by another reason to invest: fear. I feared having to sell my house, not being able to provide for my family, and not having a job. I feared that my job, which I devoted a significant amount of my time and effort in study, would become obsolete; I feared ending up on the street, homeless. For me, it came down to a choice: Do I follow the same path that my parents followed, or do I allow fear to be my guide and use it to move forward? Suffice to say, I moved forward and invested in my first property.

After my first investment, watching the financial structure work and seeing the property increase in value in the first year reduced the "what ifs" and a substantial amount of my fear. The way I looked at it, if something were to happen, I had an additional asset which was helping to reduce my tax; in the event that something occurred, I had something I could sell and use the profits to reduce my debts and buy some time whilst I worked out my next step.

The next step was to look more closely at my property investment approach. One investment property was good, and two was better, but it certainly did not generate enough cash flow to sustain me in the long term (although it did give me a few more options). It certainly seemed like a pathway for me to move towards, and so my investment approach changed, and I transitioned from investing as a way to reduce my fears and concerns about the future to what I saw as a way to build wealth that could sustain me for the long term. Some of the other stories I heard focused on building wealth through buying properties, renovating them, and flipping them for profit; whilst this can be lucrative, it can consume a considerable amount of time. I decided to take an approach that was more gradual, where I set myself a goal to purchase one property a year, every year, and select a mix of properties that were geared towards capital growth as well as cash flow.

I mentioned that I have a group of like-minded friends who like to invest. One friend lives in the northern suburbs in a two-bedroom house on a large size block. The house itself is roughly 12 squares and is a late 1950s/early 1960s property, which he had renovated some years ago. He has a family with two teenage kids.

A few years ago, we were talking about investing in property, and he told me he had finally purchased an investment property in St Kilda (located on the outskirts of the Melbourne Central Business District; it has beachfront areas, as well as a vibrant restaurant scene). He bought an apartment there, off the plan, for roughly $630,000. In addition, the property was rented for the first year at $350 a week, and his accountant said he's able to get a tax deduction, which he was happy with.

When I did the sums in my head, however, I saw that for the money he put down, he could have purchased two properties in Geelong; combined, they would have yielded a higher return. I didn't want to rain on his parade, as he was obviously really happy with his purchase, but I asked what he thought about some of the up-and-coming suburbs.

He gave me a funny look and said, "You don't understand; it's St Kilda. I've always wanted to live in St Kilda."

I said, "OK, so is your long-term plan to move into this property and live there?"

He responded that he couldn't afford to live in the area; later on, after his kids moved out of home, he was actually thinking about moving overseas to a place with a warmer climate.

I did understand. His motive wasn't wealth creation, nor was the investment driven by fear. He invested in the property for its prestige and to keep up appearances. This was something I hadn't thought about. He seemed happy, and the property gave him what he was looking for, so I congratulated him on his purchase.

I knew that his kids were the same age as my two children, and I wondered what it would be like for them when their kids finally moved out and looked for a place of their own to live in. From what my parents told me about their struggles with buying their own home, it seemed simpler than the issues I had. For instance, when they bought their first home, they paid roughly sixteen thousand dollars for a house and land package. At the time, their combined income was around nine thousand dollars. So their house cost roughly two times their annual income. When I purchased my first home, the total cost of the property was around $200,000, and my combined income was around $51,000. This was roughly 3.9 times my annual income. Today, on average, the average annual income is around $86,000, and house prices are around $737,000. This is around 8.6 times the annual income. What is apparent here is that the average house price is increasing faster than the average pay rates. So it is a safe bet that by the time my children are ready to move out, housing costs will be far beyond what their income could support.

This means they have three options:

1. They could rent forever.
2. They could move out to a more rural location, where houses are cheaper.
3. They could lock themselves into a debt they'll spend years trying to pay off.

I didn't like the idea of option 3, as they would have to take on a high level of risk and earn more than the average wage just to qualify for a loan. Option 2 is more reasonable costwise, but we wouldn't see our children as often (nor grandchildren, if and when they came along). Option 1 is viable, but would it give them the security and comfort that I now enjoy?

There is one other option, which some families do, and I think it may become more common in the years ahead. That is, the kids never move out; they stay with the parents, and as the family grows, the parents and children both go for a loan together and pool their resources to build a larger home that accommodates the entire family.

I thought about this and realised how difficult it could be, not only for my kids to have their own properties, but also for the generations that follow them. Having your own home, let alone investing in property, may become something few people get the chance to do; they either rent a place to live, never leave home at all, or wait for an inheritance of some sort. So for me, another reason for investing in property is to leave something behind of use to the generations that follow. I guess you could call it a legacy.

So to sum things up, people invest in a property due to fear, wealth creation, security, prestige, and legacy.

10

Step 1: Budget and Finance

When my friends and I discuss money and property, the conversations are often quite robust; we debate what to do and which investment is the better way to go. However, we all agree on one thing: where to start. Before you look at property, before you look at banks or brokers, the first thing that needs to be done is to create a budget and set up a structure to actively track your spending. Most people roll their eyes when I talk about budgets and tracking their spending. I've had people tell me it's boring. They ask, "What does a budget have to do with an investment property?"

I cannot stress enough how important it was for me to know how much I was spending on a daily, weekly, monthly, and annual basis; I also set controls in place to ensure that I had some flexibility. To me, these are the foundation blocks to building wealth. Similar to laying a concrete foundation for a house, setting up a budget and tracking spending is the unseen side to investment. But it is necessary, as without it, you are effectively running blind, with no way to determine if what you are doing is working for you. There is no way to gauge if you can afford certain expenses.

You will have money coming in from your investment property and also money going out to support and maintain it. Without having the structure to track this, you'll be unable to track what is going on, but come the end of the year, it will be a stressful exercise to accumulate all the data your accountant needs.

I have friends who own their home and also an investment property. They have had their investment property for a number of years, and its value has gone up considerably, which they're happy about. Recently, they looked into getting an additional property; they loved the idea of expanding their portfolio so they'd have a bigger nest egg for the future. However, they weren't sure how to do it, as they had minimal savings for a deposit. They weren't sure how this new purchase would impact their cash flow and family commitments, but they really wanted to purchase a new property. They were at a point in life where they understood they needed money to fund their retirement and were unsure if the government would be able to support their pensions by the time they reach retirement age. Hence, they wanted to increase their investment portfolio so they had more options down the road. As for the type of property, they wanted a property that was geared for capital growth, as it would give them something to use later on.

I understand wanting to have something for later and building wealth through property that increases in value. But what if the property costs more than you are prepared to spend? What if you have to sell it? What if the property is not rented for a period of time? Budgeting and tracking tools address these issues at the earliest point in time.

I tend to buy properties at what my broker tells me is a faster-than-normal rate. To do this, I developed some documents which have made it easier for me to budget and track my spending. The first document is an income and outgoing spreadsheet which charts out progress over the course of the week and month.

October Projection

INCOME

date	4th		11th		18th		25th	
Pay	$		Pay	$	Pay	$	Pay	$
VIC Rentals	$	VIC Rentals	$	VIC Rentals	$	VIC Rentals	$
NSW Rentals	$	NSW Rentals	$	NSW Rentals	$	NSW Rentals	$
QLD Rentals	$	QLD Rentals	$	QLD Rentals	$	QLD Rentals	$
	$		$		$		$
	$		$		$		$
	$		$		$		$
	$		$		$		$
	$		$		$		$
income	$		$		$		$
							TOTAL	$0.00

OUTGOINGS

date	4th		11th		18th		25th	
Loans	$	Loans	$	Loans	$	Loans	$
VIC Rates	$	VIC Rates	$	VIC Rates	$	VIC Rates	$
NSW Rates	$	NSW Rates	$	NSW Rates	$	NSW Rates	$
QLD Rates	$	QLD Rates	$	QLD Rates	$	QLD Rates	$
VIC Water Charges	$	VIC Water Charges	$	VIC Water Charges	$	VIC Water Charges	$
NSW Water Charges	$	NSW Water Charges	$	NSW Water Charges	$	NSW Water Charges	$
QLD Water Charges	$	QLD Water Charges	$	QLD Water Charges	$	QLD Water Charges	$
VIC Insurance	$	VIC Insurance	$	VIC Insurance	$	VIC Insurance	$
NSW Insurance	$	NSW Insurance	$	NSW Insurance	$	NSW Insurance	$
QLD Insurance	$	QLD Insurance	$	QLD Insurance	$	QLD Insurance	$
	$		$		$		$
	$		$		$		$
	$		$		$		$
	$		$		$		$
							TOTAL	0

Monthly Revenue	$
Monthly Outgoings	$
monthly savings	$

My document looks like the template above. In addition to the property elements, I also add all personal spending so I have a true understanding of how much money I have available. I make a game of it, where the goal is to always be in the positive for monthly savings. This document may seem crude to those used to a profit-and-loss statement, but it works for me.

I also use a property projection document, which allows me to look at a property and include all the running costs and rental return. This helps me to understand exactly what the costs associated for a new property is. I then take the total outgoings and income for a particular property and add it into the first spreadsheet. This then gives me a good understanding as to how this property will perform and what it will mean when it is added into the group of properties I currently have.

Below is my property review spreadsheet, which I use to assess a property.

Broken Hill Property		
PROCUREMENT		
Procurement cost	$	75,000.00
stamp duty	$	7,000.00
converyancing	$	660.00
incidentals	$	1,000.00
deposit	$	15,000.00
TOTAL	$	68,660.00
RENTAL RETURN		
Rent	$	**680.00**
Raywhite		
OUTGOINGS		
Agent Management	$	54.40
rates	$	79.17
water	$	87.50
loan projection	$	253.00
Insurance	$	30.20
"What if" redraw budget	$	50.00
TOTAL	$	554.27
Monthly Cash Flow	$	125.74

In terms of outgoings, I have found there really are only a few. The first is the loan payment. To get an understanding of this, I use online tools that the banks provide to calculate loan repayments. One of my favourites also allows you to input your own interest rate, which can be useful to calculate current repayments and calculate what amount of money the loan could require to support the investment property, should interest rates rise or fall, or should I choose to refinance.

The next charge to expect is for water. On my first investment property, I questioned this, as the rental agreement stated that the tenant would pay for the water. So I found it odd that three months after I bought the property, I received a bill from the water company. The agent explained that the tenant only pays for the water usage. However, the landlord pays for other charges, such as sewage charges, administration fees, and maintenance.

Tax rates are another charge you can expect; they come every three months and often go up when the value of the property is reassessed. You can pay annually or quarterly, which I prefer, as the costs are the same, and it helps with my cash flow.

Landlord's insurance is self-explanatory. Unlike rates and water, this is something you have a degree of control over. I shop around; whilst a number of insurance companies are serviced by a common underwriter, there can be variations in the market, as well as variations depending on how much you choose to insure the property for, the level that you set the excess for, the extras you select, and how you choose to pay. I take a minimalist approach to insurance. I see it as something you spend money on but hope you never want to use. To reduce the cost of insurance, I look at paying annually as opposed to monthly and taking out only the coverage that make sense to me. For instance, if a property is in a flood zone, then it makes sense to take flood coverage. But if it's in a desert or has had minimal water over the last fifty-plus years, then it's possible to take a risk and not have flood coverage.

Another element I look at is the excess. I tend to set this as high as possible. Then, for small issues such as a broken window, I choose to pay for that to be fixed out of my own pocket, as opposed to claiming it on insurance. In addition, I look for companies that offer multipolicy discounts and shift my insurance policies, depending on what company gives me the most value for my money.

The final outgoing cost is repairs and maintenance. This is part and parcel of having any type of property. Over time, things wear down and require work being carried out. Some examples are tap washers, clogged drains or toilets, broken electrical switches, and doors that jam in summer as a result of expansion due to heat. As a landlord, you will need to have funds available for this or have the agent pay for them out of the rental return. Every month for each property, I set aside a nominal figure, which varies depending on the type of property. For instance, I set aside a lower figure for newer properties and more for older properties. I park these funds in the redraw of the property, where it works against the interest. Then when something happens, be it a wear-and-tear issue or a low-cost breakage, I use these funds to pay for whatever needs to be done.

I should point out that with the outgoings, it's not all doom and gloom. These expenses are deductible, and I can claim them when I do my tax return. I look at outgoings as levers. Some of them, such as tax rates and water costs, you can't move; others, though, like insurance, loan repayments, and repairs and maintenance budgets can be manipulated, to a degree. By adjusting these levers, I can determine if a property is to be negatively or positively geared.

The other side to this is income. This is another lever that can be manipulated. For instance, depending on the location, demand on a property, and time till the lease agreement is due, I can ask for more or less rent. Similarly, if a property has been renovated or has additional features, such as dishwashers or solar panels, these items can be depreciated, and they are things that prospective renters see as desirable. Prospective tenant may be willing to pay a slightly higher rent to have them.

As you can see, there is so much more to an investment property than just buying a house in a good area that has access to good services. Whilst these help, it's vital to have the structures in place to understand what the property is doing, what benefits they provide, how much it earns, but more importantly how much is left over after each month.

I use these documents to help me understand the nature of an investment property. In addition, as the information in the tracking documents builds up over time, it also gives me the information I need to predict what I need to do in the future. For instance, for my property in Geelong, over the past four winters, the storm water drain has become blocked after heavy rain. This has resulted in a visit from a plumber, who sent down a tool to clean and cut some roots that have grown and blocked a section of pipe. The pipe is old and has cracked over the years; these cracks allow the tree roots to enter in and grow. This costs roughly $350 a visit.

However, the cost to replace the section of pipe was around $1700, as it also involves a bit of work to excavate. With this data available, I am able to make an informed decision. I know that if I was to have the pipe replaced, it would take roughly five years for it to essentially pay for itself. Knowing I intend to keep the property for a long time made my decision easy: I had the section of pipe replaced with funds that had been stored in the redraw.

By having this level of detail and information available on the properties I own and by understanding what levers exist with each property, I can look at the result if I played with the levers on the income and outgoing of the property. In some instances, by playing with these levers, I am able to influence the type of property I have and have them run as a negative geared property or transition from negative geared to a property which is cash flow positive.

11

Cash Flow Positive

After watching my properties operate over the interest-only period, I realised they didn't require any additional funding to run, which was great. However, after the interest-only period ended, the repayments increased. This was due to the terms of the loan; specifically, the loan period did not change, so the only way to make up for the reduction in principal repayments that had accrued over the one-year period was to increase the overall repayments to compensate, which would ensure that the loan would be complete on the due date.

It occurred to me that the ideal position would be to have a property that paid for itself in a similar way to how my properties paid for themselves when they were in an interest-only state, but without the issues associated with being in that setup. This is called a cash flow positive property; it's when a property is making enough money to pay for all of the outgoings, with something left over. Unless investors are already wealthy, they require a loan in order to invest in a property. Whether the loan is principal-and-interest or interest-only, as you have seen in the tracking documents, the loan payment is the largest outgoing for the investment property. For a principal-and-interest loan, with some playing with the levers on hand, the loan amount can reduce and opportunities may be created where the repayment amount for the property also reduces. This results in the property going from a negative geared investment to a positive geared property.

All the properties I acquired up until 2014 were negatively geared. However, even though the property in Horsham was a recent purchase, it came pretty close to being positively geared and cost me roughly sixty dollars a month to support. It occurred to me that if a recent purchase could be close to positively geared from day one, perhaps it was possible to procure properties that were designed for this purpose.

So I set to the task. I needed to find something where the running costs were lower than the rental return. To get the running costs such as loan, insurance, water, and rates to a point where they were less than the rental return, I needed a property with a high rental return. I first considered a new property. However, the cost associated with purchasing land and then constructing the house, as well as the loss incurred while the house was being built, did not make this a viable option. The only way this could work would be by constructing a large number of properties on the site, which would provide the rental income required to make it a positive investment. Whilst this would have been a great project to carry out, I wasn't in a position to raise the funds required to try this, so I decided against this option.

The alternative option was to look for an existing property which, when procured, was instantly cash flow positive. I searched across Melbourne and didn't limit myself to just houses; I searched all property types. Within Melbourne, I couldn't find anything, so I started to look farther out and finally came upon the town of Warracknabeal. This location was relatively close to Horsham, but with a much smaller population. It had roughly twenty-five hundred people. The town had been around since the 1800s, so it certainly wasn't going anywhere, and the vacancy rate was under 1 per cent The average price for a property was seventy thousand dollars, and the average rental return was around $175 per week.

After some searching, I came across a three-bedroom property with a large garage; it had a long rental history, leased for $170 per week, and seemed to be in good condition. I made an initial offer for sixty thousand dollars. After some negotiation, I finally picked up the property for sixty-five thousand dollars. Settlement for the property took ninety days to complete. With the volume of lending, the bank had no issue with providing funding for this one.

You might ask why I selected this property. Well, at the time, a cash flow positive property was a new concept to me, and there wasn't a lot of literature on the subject. In fact, at that time, most of the information around property investment was on negative gearing. So this property was to be a test, to see if it was indeed possible to purchase a cash flow positive property.

Once the property cleared and was under my control, I added it to my tracking spreadsheet and started to monitor it. Over the course of the year, I tracked the outgoings and compared it to the return. I found that the property actually managed to generate a return of $1,440 for the year. Whilst this was not a huge amount, it certainly proved that it was indeed possible to source a property that would be cash flow positive from the moment it was purchased.

12

Negative Gear versus Cash Flow Positive

I now had two types of properties: negative geared properties and a cash flow positive property. Each of these are very different, and they both have their place and do certain things.

The negative geared properties, whilst not making a profit, are in locations where the value of the land is appreciating over time. This creates wealth for me in terms of capital growth as time goes by. They also allow me to claim a tax deduction, and the equity in them is useful for securing further funding.

The cash flow positive property, on the other hand, produces profit. However, this one is in a location where the land value wasn't high to begin with, nor was it expected to increase rapidly. However, the returns pay all of the outgoings, and I am left with some cash at the end, which is useful when approaching a bank for further lending, as it's considered as income.

So if we add, say, ten years to each of these options and work on the premise that the properties do what I predict they will do, I get two different outcomes. From the negative geared property, the rental return may go up a little over time, but it may not offset the outgoings. However, the value of the property will more than likely go up. As a result, I will have access to equity I can move into cash by selling the property itself or borrowing against it.

If the value of the positive geared property increases over the ten-year period, that's great; the property will generate a stable income and yield a small income. So the effort required to support it is less; when a bank looks at this type of property, it's considered an income stream. This is useful when securing additional loans or paying off existing debts.

Ultimately, deciding which type of property to go after is something that only the investor can make, as they understand their personal situation and know what they are looking to achieve.

For me, I see positive geared and negative geared properties as similar to good and bad cholesterol, respectively. If I have too many negative geared properties, then my borrowing capacity drops, and I cannot borrow more money from the bank. However, with the positive and negatively geared properties carefully balanced and working with each other, I can build my property portfolio without having to land a higher paying job or changing my lifestyle.

13

Mining Towns

Many towns in Australia were built as a result of mining. Most of these towns were established around the mid-1800s. Whilst some closed after the mining boom ended and became ghost towns, a number remained and now have a vibrant community and some beautiful period-style homes. Some of the more notable towns are Ballarat, Broken Hill, and Coober Pedy.

In 2015, I wanted to expand my cash flow positive portfolio but didn't have access to large amounts of funding, so I needed to be precise and calculated. I had looked at Horsham, in the state of Victoria, before, and decided to start with this area again. To my surprise, property values in the area had gone up since the last time I looked at them. On the one hand, this was good, as it meant the assets I purchased there had now gone up in value. On the downside, though, these properties were still a considerably good value, when compared with properties of similar size in Melbourne. That increase in value meant that any future property procured in this location wouldn't immediately go cash flow positive, but would be negative for at least five years.

Next, I expanded my search into other states. The criteria I set was a budget of $80k for a property, land size of 500 metres square, and a minimum of three bedrooms. At the top of the list was a property in Broken Hill. Up until that point, the only thing I knew about Broken Hill was that it is the home for BHP. So I started to look more closely at this area. I found that it was indeed the home of BHP. The town itself had a population of roughly nineteen thousand people. At the peak of the mining industry, the population reached thirty-five thousand. However, mining in Broken Hill had long since ceased, and over time, the population had halved. I was about to pass on this area and look elsewhere; however, I saw that it was still one of the largest rural towns in New South Wales.

It also had a thriving art community, film industry, and planning for one of the largest solar farms in Australia. I considered the situation and wondered why these organisations had invested in the town. The only reason I could think of was that they could see value and a future for the town. Based on this, I thought I would try and purchase a positive geared property here. After speaking to a number of agents, I found two properties that seemed a good fit. Both were three-bedroom houses. One was going for seventy-five thousand dollars and the other for sixty-eight thousand dollars. In addition to this, both properties were rented. One was leased for $230, and the other was leased for $160 a week. It was quite a large difference between the two properties in terms of rental return, but they seemed to return more money than it would cost to support the loan and other running costs for these properties.

At the time, I thought I must be missing something here. This certainly seemed too good to be true. At that point, I started thinking about the two words I hate most in the world: What if? What if the town shrank further? What if the value of the property continued to fall? What if the rental market there dried up? What if I missed something? I thought about this for a while and then thought about the inverse: What if I did nothing? What if the value went up? What if I missed the opportunity?

Whilst I do hate those two words, they actually do serve a purpose, which is to help balance out the decisions I make. After thinking about these two opportunities and running the numbers through my spreadsheet, I heard the voice in my head, which I had not heard for quite a while, say, "Shut up and do it."

With that in mind, I went back to the agents for these properties and put in an offer for ten thousand dollars less than the advertised price. This was not due to me thinking the price was too low. It was based on understanding that all agents set a price range. In a location such as this, there are risks. These risks may put off some prospective investors, hence my thought process was the asking price they suggested might be a midpoint of their range. Therefore, by going in under the asking value, if it's accepted, that would be great; if it isn't, then it simply sets the starting place for negotiation.

Both offers were rejected; however, the feedback with the lower priced property was that we were close. As for the $75k property, this was a firm no, and the feedback was that the seller was happy to hang on until the right purchaser came along. I have learnt that feedback is very important in any negotiation, as it's a window into what the seller may be thinking. This is not an exact science, it's more an art form, but from the two responses, I did the following:

I offered $60k for the house that listed for $68k. My thought was that it was in the $10k range the seller was looking for, and given all the what ifs, they may be inclined to accept the offer. As for the other property, the feedback suggested they were in a comfortable position. The real estate agent, no matter what, would want to make a sale. So the route I went down was to annoy the agent. I increased my offer by $500, which was rejected. I then added another $250 and submitted it to the agent. This was also rejected; however, this time, they came back with a counteroffer of $70k. I then added another $500 to the deal, which was rejected. By this point, the agent was getting frustrated, as each time I made an offer, they needed to take it to the owner. This process took up time and resources.

Finally, the agent asked whether I was serious about purchasing the property. I responded, "Yes, and depending on how we go with this property, I may purchase more in the area." I then told him I would make another offer after checking my finances and would get back to him the next day. This approach allowed me to gauge how many other buyers were out there for this particular property (the agent never said there were other offers, which suggested that I was the only bidder).

The agent actually called me the following morning to ask if I would like to make an offer (this confirmed my suspicion that I was the only bidder). My thought was, if there was interest for this property, then the agent, knowing to expect small increments from me, would have focused on following up with bids from other bidders. This and the fact that the seller had already dropped the price by $5k gave me the strong impression that we simply needed to get the seller down to a point where they would be worn out and take their minimum price. So with that in mind, I made another bid, adding an extra hundred dollars to the offer. The seller not only rejected the offer but said they weren't in the mood to constantly go back and forth. They'd only entertain a serious offer.

So I made a final offer of $67,000 and agreed to a one-month settlement, subject to finance and an independent building inspection. The agent took that to the seller. I didn't hear back from the agent for forty-eight hours. When they did call, they only had two words for me: "Offer accepted." Obviously, I was quite pleased and asked them to send through the paperwork so we could get moving.

Both properties had an independent building inspection carried out. I have found these to be useful, especially when buying older properties, to help gain an understanding of what issues I might be up for and have to budget for in the future or simply for removing some of the what ifs from the decision-making process.

As soon as these two properties were purchased, I added them to my tracking spreadsheet and started to monitor them. After three months, they proved the concept that is was possible to source a cash flow positive property and return more money than they cost to run.

14

Currency

What is cash? It goes by many names: legal tender, banknotes, hard cash, dough, bread, and my favourite, cheddar. Whatever you call it, these days, it's simply a piece of paper that represents value. A very long time ago, people used to carry gold. However, this was not a very secure option, nor was it the most practical solution for large purchases. So people stored their money in secured locations, banks, who would then provide them with something written down that represented how much gold they had. Over time, these banknotes became more uniform, and people started to simply trade the banknotes. As for the gold, well, that remained in the bank. The benefit of this system was that it controlled the economy of a country, as the volume of gold it had grew based upon trade and its ability to mine the precious mineral.

It was not until the Great Depression of the 1930s that the link to gold was tested in the United States. During this period, a number of countries suffered record unemployment, and their economies came to a halt. People started to cash out their deposits in banks, which depleted the gold reserves. The government's only option was to raise interest rates; however, doing this would have placed even greater pressure on businesses. So a number of countries decided to cut their ties to the gold standard, which allowed them to pump more money into the economy.

This did impact the value of the dollar against other countries, but with more money circulating around it, encouraged people to spend, which then kick-started the economy into action. So in essence, the government spent its way out of the depression.

Why is this important? Up until that point, the value of gold dictated the value of all of goods and services. Property, being one of these goods, moved at a slow rate, largely dictated by the scarcity of the precious metal. However, once this link was disconnected, the value of property as well as goods and services could shift more freely.

I treat currency like energy. It is a power source that funds my dreams and moves me forward. Also, like energy, once created, you either put it to use or store it. But when it is stored, the value only lasts for a period and degrades over time. However, if the energy created is put into creating something else, this is where the highest value is derived from it, as what it creates becomes more valuable over time.

15

Subdivisions

This is something that is becoming more common. People who own large blocks of land are subdividing them into smaller blocks, that can then have multiple dwellings built on them. The property I bought in Geelong, where I installed my uncle's kitchen, was bought with the intent of subdividing. I selected this property for subdivision because of its size. It was close to 700 metres square. Why does that matter? Well, in the state of Victoria, the minimum block size that you can subdivide is 600 metres square. If you want to subdivide a property smaller than this, you need to seek permission from the Victorian Builders Association (VBA) and make a good case for doing so. These rules, however, vary from state to state.

This particular caveat was something I learnt from a good friend of mine, who had been investing in property for longer than I had. He would purchase a property in a suburb, move into the house, and then carry out some minor renovations. Then once the value of property increased, he would sell it and move on to another area. I saw him use this approach in Airport West, then in Moonee Ponds, and finally in Avondale Heights.

In Avondale Heights, he bought a two-bedroom property on a corner block with the intention of subdividing the backyard to build a townhouse to live in and then renting out the house, which he was in the process of renovating. Once he completed his renovation, he applied for a subdivision of the block. He completed the paperwork for his block and submitted it to council. After a few weeks, he received a rejection letter. The reason for rejection was due to the size of the land. His block was 594 square metres, just 6 square metres short of minimum 600 square metres.

This information about the minimum land size required for subdivision was certainly helpful for me with the Geelong property. It helped make the selection process clearer, and as a result, I knew for certain that it would meet the size requirement. The property I had selected was a corner block. The reasoning behind this was that corner blocks have two sides to the block that face a street. This gives more options for creating driveways and placing properties on the land that are street-facing. This might not mean much, but any property which has common lands or driveways needs to have a body corporate set up, to ensure that these aspects are looked after. This adds cost and in some cases might reduce the desirability of the property.

I wanted to do something similar to what my friend had intended to do in Avondale Heights, where the existing dwelling on the property is retained and the backyard area subdivided in preparation for constructing a new property. What I did next was to source a survey and consulting group, to assist with the subdivision. With a subdivision, there is a substantial amount of paperwork and survey work required. The brief provided was to look at a subdivision for at least two subdivisions. As part of the survey, the existing structure was reviewed. It turned out that the site was subdividable; however, the existing dwelling was too close to the centre of the block, which meant it would need to be demolished. In addition to this, the survey team also cross-checked with the water board and found that the wastewater services were too small to support two properties. The fix for this was to run an additional line for storm water and sewage from the property out to the street. Whilst this sounds relatively easy, in practice, it requires excavating trenches and running them out to the road. It would also result in the tearing up part of the road to access the main sewer and storm water lines. Initial cost estimates for this were around $95,000. At the time, a block of land in that area went for $80k. So to make long story short, subdividing that property was technically feasible but not cost-effective.

I decided to continue it as a rental and keep the survey data stored for a later date, when the value of the land in that area reached a point where it made sense to subdivide.

I learnt a few things from this. Firstly, if you think a property you want to purchase today is something you want to subdivide in the future, speak to a survey company that specialises in subdivisions to get an overview on what is required. Keep in mind that these companies do charge for their assistance, so you do need to be certain about what your intent is.

I also learnt that the water board kept detailed files on each property and can be a great source of information and assistance. For the property I was considering, if I asked the water board if the property could service multiple dwellings, they could have told me.

16

Relocated Homes

In early 2017, I noticed more and more subdivisions going on in Horsham. I noticed a block from realestate.com.au that was roughly 590 square metres, a flat block that had all services ready to go, including fencing installed. The price was really what got my attention: twenty-six thousand dollars. This seemed too good too be true, so one Saturday afternoon, I took the entire family on a trip to Horsham. The trip was three and a half hours through the country. The only sound that could be heard was the radio and a voice from the back seat, saying, "Are we there yet?"

About three hundred kilometres later and what seemed like all day in the car, we finally reached Horsham. I had been in communication with the real estate agent. As the property was a vacant block, it was quite easy to inspect. The property was in an older part of Horsham, relatively close to the centre of town. The flat block of land was fenced off, but one of the fences was damaged and appeared to have been burnt by a fire. There was a water meter at the front of the property and a sewer inspection manhole in the rear; a small garden shed was installed over the manhole.

As I was poking around the block, the next-door neighbour came over to say hello. He was quite friendly, and I soon found out that the block of land once had a house on it, but it burnt down a year ago. The neighbour told me the owner received an insurance payout and was looking to get rid of the property, as it was costing him a little bit to maintain.

I thanked the neighbour for the information and drove off to look more closely at the area. This block of land was located within a small pocket of properties that were built in the 1950s and 1960s. As I got back onto the main road, I could see some development in the distance. I decided to take a closer look and found new roads, infrastructure, and new blocks of land that were on the market, with a starting price of sixty thousand dollars. In contrast, the block of land I looked at seemed like a good buy.

I contacted the agent and asked for the Section 32 for the property, which confirmed that what I had seen was a manhole for the sewer. The property didn't have any caveats or issues that could impact whether a house could be constructed on the site.

I put in an offer for twenty thousand dollars for this property. This was rejected, and the owner came back with a counteroffer of twenty-three thousand dollars. I then offered twenty-one thousand dollars, with a one-month settlement and no subject to finance. This was accepted by the agent within ten minutes of the offer.

So now I had purchased a block of land that I believed to be undervalued. The next objective was to work out what I was going to do with this property. I could have simply held onto it and waited for the value of the land to go up. I could have found a builder and had a house built upon it. I gave some serious thought to this approach. It was tried and true, predictable, and something I understood well.

However, I thought about alternative options. The two options I had in mind were to build a kit home or to relocate a house onto the site. I did like the idea of a kit home, but the idea of taking something that was going to end up as waste and upcycling it into something of value greatly appealed to me. So I went down the relocation option. After using Google to review a number of websites, I found a local provider who specialised in providing houses that were looking for new blocks of land to reside on. They had a wide range of properties, from single- to double-story houses in all shapes and sizes. This was my first dabble into this type of investment, and at the end of the day, the property was to become a rental. I wanted to see just how cheaply I could develop it.

The cheapest house listed was a small two-bedroom weatherboard that was located in Glen Waverly. The asking price was sixty-four thousand dollars. The seller offered an inspection of the property prior to purchase, which I took them up on. It was a 1940s bungalow. The property was small and pokey. The kitchen and bathroom had been updated in the 1990s and was a pastel pink. The lounge was L shaped. It seemed like a good enough house to start with, so after a little negotiation, I purchased it.

The next step was to commence the paperwork. I needed to apply for an owner builder's license from the Victorian Builders Association, so I could oversee the work required. In addition, an approval was needed to demolish the property on the existing block of land in Glen Waverly and approved architectural building plans as well as the relevant permits to have the house installed onto its new block of land in Horsham.

The company providing the property applied for the relevant paperwork to have the house removed from its current location and reinstated in the new location. About six weeks after we signed all the papers, we took down the roof, cut the house into two sections, and loaded them onto two trucks for transport all the way to Horsham. At the Horsham end, builders were onsite to drill holes for posts and get things in place for when the house arrived.

This is where we encountered a small issue. Whilst the block of land was flat, about half a metre down, the builders encountered construction and part of the foundations from the old property. This made it difficult for the builders to drill through, as the bricks and concrete damaged the drill bits. However, with some extra drill bits, they were able to create the number of post holes required before the house arrived.

Two large trucks drove up to the property, each containing one half of the house. The tradespeople then spent much of the day carefully manoeuvring the halves of the house into place with a series of hydraulic jacks. Once the sections were in place, they were joined back together and posts were connected to the underside of the house and cemented into the predug post holes. The foundations were left to dry for roughly twenty-four hours, after which the jacks were removed. The roof frame was then reinstalled, and as a last step, tarps were put over the roof frames to protect the house from rain.

The trip down for the house was quite long and bumpy, and whilst the company providing the service did everything they could to ensure the house arrived as intact as possible, there were a number of cracks in the plaster boards. To offset this, they kindly offered four thousand dollars back. However, I had a different thought. As the weight of the roof was removed, I asked if they could install a laminated veneer lumber (LVL) roof that would run the length of the house and allow the removal of two walls that divided the kitchen, entry, and lounge, which they agreed to do. This then meant that the pokey little house would become an open plan property.

After the work to install the LVL, the house was then mine to finish off. No DIY could have prepared me for what work was ahead of me. There were sections of the house that were open to the elements, gaps in the flooring where the two sections of the house were joined, and a hole where a fireplace used to be. Out of all the items that needed to be done, the most important was to make sure the house was watertight. I started with the roof. The house originally had terracotta tiles; however,

I opted for a metal roof, as it was cheaper and quicker to install. This required a carpenter and a plumber. The carpenter installed the battens onto the roof to hold the metal and also facia boards, which needed to be installed before the roof itself went on. The battens and facia boards went on quite quickly and easily.

The metal roof, on the other hand, took a bit longer. This was mainly due to the weather in Horsham, which turned cold and rainy just after the battens were installed. It took close two weeks to finally close in the roof. It would have been quicker to have the carpenter carry out the work, but this was not possible. Due to certification and compliance issues, a plumber had to do it. The roof needed to be installed by a plumber, who could ensure that it is watertight, as well as ensuring how the roof deals with any water that falls onto it.

Once the roof was installed, there was only one area that was open to the weather, which was a section of wall where the chimney had been. This was the first time I could actually use some of my skills to put in a timber frame and then insulate and close up the wall space, which finally brought the property up to lockup stage. There was one little issue, though. Whilst all of the tradespeople had worked as quickly as possible, water managed to get past the temporary tarps and onto the ceiling plaster, cracking it. A few taps with a stick, and a large section of plaster came down.

From this, I learnt a couple of things. Firstly, hard hats are really, really good things to wear when working on a construction site, and secondly, whilst some plaster boards were in good condition, it would have been easier in the long term to remove all of it from the walls and floor, rather then trying to save some of the good sections.

The next major issue I encountered was the window frames at the back of the house. Before the house was relocated, they appeared to be fine. However, after a bit of vibration, the timber had worked its way free. After looking at the frames in closer detail, the reason for them working their way free was timber rot. What made this even more of an issue was that these frames were not off-the-shelf frames, nor were they completely square. They appeared to be homemade frames that were probably made to enclose a rear veranda and turn it into more usable space.

I tried to see if we could retain some of them, but from my lessons learnt with the ceiling, the easier and better long-term solution was to remove the old windows and install new ones. This, though, presented me with a new challenge. Where do I go to get a twenty-first-century equivalent of these windows? Also, the new windows created an issue with the plans submitted to council. My first call was to the draftsman, to ask about options. His response was as I thought: If the type of window is changed, then it would require the design of the property to be reviewed; the drawings needed to be amended and then submitted to council for approval. If approved, the window frames could be changed. The alternative was to rebuild the window frames to the same dimensions and design as the ones that failed. A bespoke replacement would cost more than an off-the-shelf option, but it would save time and cost in the design process. I chose the bespoke replacement option. Whilst it was costly, it was a known cost, and the result was a known outcome.

Now that the outside of the house was watertight, I could start on the inside. I planned to rent the house, so the level of finish needed to be good but also needed to be hard wearing. The other factor I thought about was, now that two walls had been removed, the entry, kitchen, and lounge became one big open space. It seemed more than enough for a family space, so I thought creatively and sectioned the L-shaped lounge off into a rectangle; this allowed me to create another room, which turned the property from a two bedroom into a three-bedroom home. To do this was quite simple and involved building an internal wall frame.

Whilst I was doing this, I also took the opportunity to create some built-in cupboards and study nooks for each bedroom. I also had electricians in, to rough in all the wiring for light fittings and power points and had a plumber run all the plumbing services. I used the same plumber who installed the roof, and he also provided a wealth of knowledge about which tradespeople to use to connect all of the electrical services and do the plastering, insulation, and general labouring work.

Once electricity and plumbing were installed, I installed plasterboards onto the new walls as well as the ceilings. To do the ceilings required the hiring of a tilt lift, which I found very helpful to lift the lengths of material up onto the ceilings and position it correctly. The other thing that I patted myself on the back for, was to buy and leave all of the insulation bats in the ceiling, ready to install once the plasterboards was in place. This actually saved so much time. Installing the plasterboards was relatively easy. However, doing cornices and plastering up the joins was a skill set I didn't have. I got a skilled tradesperson in to carry this work out, which took them no time at all to do. I then had the electricians back in to fit the power points and light fittings and prepare the meter box to be connected to street power.

Finally, power was connected to the site. This meant that I didn't have to run extension leads from next door or run floodlights. This allowed work to carry on well after 5 p.m.; I could work late painting the walls and ceilings with primer and then colour. After the painting was done, it was time to do the flooring. The house had timber floors, but it also had sections with joins visible, as a result of the relocation. I decided to install carpets in the bedrooms and laminated timber flooring in the living areas.

The house was now almost ready for a certificate of occupancy. This is the final approval from the local town planners that would allow people to move into the house. With the relocation of the house, my overriding intent was to see if it was eco friendly and cost competitive. From an eco perspective, we reused the frame, windows, bathroom, kitchen, and laundry fittings, as well as the external cladding. Including the land and insurance, the total cost of the property was $115,000. The internal size of the house is 175 square metres. If I had a builder construct a house from scratch, I would expect to pay around $1,180 per square metre. This would be a total cost of $206,500. So I guess this type of construction did achieve my goal.

Now for some of the lessons learnt with this property. The first lesson I learnt was that the tyranny of distance proved to be a problem. Whilst the land was cheap, the distance resulted in balancing work, family commitments, and the build. This created delays and significantly slowed down the construction of the property itself. All the renovations took four years to complete.

The other lesson learnt with this initiative to get to know your tradespeople and be flexible. Often for a tradesperson, your work is one among a few jobs that they will have on, each of which is just as important as the other. However, knowing what kind of workload they have and being able to give them a timeline of when you need something done can be helpful, as it allows them to plan their time accordingly.

The final thing is to get to know the local real estate agents in the area; if possible, have them visit the site before it is fitted out. I did this just after the house was plastered. I asked the agent about the area and what parts of the property I should focus on that would make for a good rental. The feedback I received was quite useful; I learnt where to focus my efforts and what features prospective tenants would consider important. In this instance, the feedback from the agent was that bedrooms, storage space, low maintenance gardens, and good heating and cooling were the top of the list.

17

Land Banking

This is where you buy a block of land and keep it for a period of time before building on it (or selling it). If you have foresight and know exactly what you want to do with a block of land, it can reduce some of the costs of a development; you can buy a block of land when it's cheap and build on it when its value has increased.

I had one family member take this approach for their own property. At the time, they were fortunate to be living at home with their parents. They didn't have enough money to build a house, but they did have enough for a deposit on a block of land. So they bought a block in an area that was relatively close to work and family. Over the next five years, they paid down the loan on the land and also planted a few trees along the fence lines and tended to the land, by making sure the grasses and weeds on the land were always at a manageable height. The contractual agreement on the land had a clause that required a dwelling to be constructed within five years of purchase. When it got close to that time, they built a home on the land.

Taking this approach did have some advantages. Firstly, the value of the land had increased substantially over the five-year period. When they initially bought the land, it was around $200k; however, when they were ready to construct a dwelling, the value had gone up to $450k. This was a far better result as opposed to banking the money in an account and trying to purchase the land at a later point.

The other advantage was when they went to the bank for a loan, they used the land as an asset, which allowed them to borrow more, as the land became the security for the loan. The final advantage was that having this land gave them time to determine what type of dwelling to construct.

The only downside they mentioned was that for the five-year period, every two to four weeks, they had to visit the property to make sure it was maintained and kept free of rubbish.

This was an interesting way to look at developing, especially if you know what you want and are prepared to wait to get it. A few years later, I was reminded of this type of option when a friend asked me to join his buying group; they were land banking property that was currently classed as farming. They bought approximately 400 acres in bulk around the Lara area in Victoria. Each acre would then be sold off for $49k to people who joined the buying group. The buying group would then sit on the land for approximately ten years, after which they would have the area rezoned as residential. The logic around this is that after ten years, the area would have other developments building up, which would help to justify the submission to the local council to have the land rezoned to residential, which should then boost the price of the land and make it attractive to developers. After this, it would be sold off to developers, and the buying group would split the profits.

Back in the 1990s, the parents of another friend bought twenty acres that were zoned as rural land for approximately $200k. They initially kept some cattle on this land, as a means to keep the vegetation at an appropriate height. In addition to this, they would periodically select a cow for slaughter which, with the help of a freezer, provided the family with a source of meat. I watched as this family eventually built a house on this property to live in, and over time, they applied to council to have the land rezoned as residential.

The population grew in this location, due to other housing developments, and the rezoned land came to the attention of a developer, who purchased the land for approximately $6.5 million. However, my friend's parents added a few interesting caveats. The first one was that they wanted to retain the area that they built their home on. The second was that once the land was subdivided and the relevant infrastructure such as roads, sewage, water, and power was established, they would own a number of blocks which would be theirs to build on or sell in later years.

I considered this as a long-term investment and liked the idea of having a large parcel of land which in future years could result in money as well as options. However, I chose not to do this. Instead, I purchased a house in Ballarat. I chose this option because I wanted my investment to work for me. To me, a vacant block of land is just that: vacant. It has minimal capacity to generate an income. Moreover, not only is the land banked, but so too are my funds, in a structure which is hard to leverage. Also, whilst I have that land banked, there are upkeep commitments, such as ensuring that it complies with whatever council requirements are applicable. For example, making sure vegetation height is kept to a certain level, to ensure that in dry seasons the risk of fire is minimised, rates are paid for on time, as well as making sure that the land is secure, which can involve the installation and upkeep of fences. All of these are outlays, few of which can be deducted.

In contrast, a property with a house on it, even an old one, generates a rental return. It is classed as an investment, so whatever is put into the maintenance and upkeep of the house is considered an outgoing cost, which can be deducted. Lastly, the house has a tenant who looks after the property and ensures that vegetation is kept to the required height. Finally, with this option, I know for certain what the land is zoned as; therefore, it doesn't matter if it's not rezoned the way I want.

18

Funding

I could write an entire book on what I have learnt about funding. There are so many ways in which to finance property investments. There is no right or wrong way to do this. When I started, I had an account with a bank that I started in childhood. When most people start out investing in property, they use the relationships they know, and it was no different in my case. I went to my bank and got a home loan for the property I lived in. In the beginning, I didn't use a broker; I did everything myself and worked with the bank to secure the funding I needed. As my investments grew, I continued working with the bank, and they started to offer more deals for me to consider. Deals such as packages designed to reduce the fees associated with procuring loans, better rates on loans and credit cards, as well as a relationship manager.

Similar to the mindset of the barefoot investor, there is no such a thing as a free lunch, and these value-added options, whilst quite useful, aren't free, and at some point, they need to be paid for.

As I mentioned earlier, I prefer principal-and-interest loans. I see loans as a lever. By shopping around, I can control my loan commitments and have an influence on whether a property is positive or negatively geared. I want to get the best deal possible. So with that in mind, I have one loan per investment. I tend to go for a variable or fixed loans with an offset/redraw account and weekly repayments.

This structure is easy for me to monitor. For instance, if a property is negatively geared and I need to calculate the interest rate. I can simply review the statements and I am done. In a combined loan structure, it can get tricky. Also if I find a better deal that works for a particular property and it makes sense to move then I can do so. The only time where I find this can be tricky is when a loan is in a fixed option, as typically I'd have to pay a penalty and fees to exit the loan.

With the offset/redraw solution, I have found the deals seem to be better in a variable loan. Under a variable loan, I get 100 per cent offset. What this means is, if I had a loan for $100k and then had $10k in the offset account, I'd be charged interest on $90k. This reduces the repayments, and I can bank more funds into the redraw or use them for other investments. If my loans were fixed, then the offset would not be 100 per cent but more like 20 to 40 per cent, which means my money wouldn't be working as hard as it could. That said, I always monitor interest rates, as it is a balancing act, and banks are forever offering new deals.

The last item was repayment cycles; I select weekly repayments because interest is calculated daily. So if I have a $100k loan and pay $400 a month, at the end of the month, your loan would be $100k plus the interest for the month, minus the repayment. But look what happens if the repayments are made weekly:

- The interest for week 1 would be calculated on $99,900.
- In week 2, it would be calculated on $99,800 plus the interest from week 1 and 2.
- In week 3, it would be calculated on $99,700 plus the interest from week 1, 2, and 3.
- In week 4, it would be calculated on $99,600 plus the interest from week 1, 2, 3, and 4.

You get the idea. With weekly repayments, I pay the same amount of money, but instead of it sitting in a bank account doing nothing until the end of the month, when it's taken out to pay the loan, it goes to work before that. This difference might not seem much. But even a small change like this would knock at least two or three years from the life of my loan, which from my perspective is money back into my pocket that I can invest in other things.

19

Step 2. Determine What Property and Location I Want

Once budgets and funding are sorted, the next step is to decide the type of property and whether it's negative geared or cash flow positive. Each option has its benefits and drawbacks; it really comes down to what I need it to achieve. However, once this is decided, it's time for the fun part: shopping.

I am constantly shopping for properties and use both realestate.com.au and domain.com.au. These websites are great online tools for reviewing property for sale in Australia; they certainly speed up my search. In addition, you can automate your searches to keep your finger on the pulse, as new properties are always coming up.

I also like the data they provide on the rental market. This information is critical, as knowing how much of a rental return you can get is key to understanding if a property is worth pursuing or not.

Once I have a property in mind, I use Google to research its location. I look for the town's population, how long it has existed, major features and industries, and rental vacancy rates. These indicators help me to gauge if a location is a good fit and assess the overall health of the property. For rural locations, I check what I call the town's "T&M," which stands for "Telstra and McDonald's." These two corporations have a significant amount of data and trend analysis.

Constructing a mobile tower or opening up a new restaurant involves a considerable amount of resources and cost. The old saying, "If you build, it they will come," may sounds nice, but in the real world, it doesn't always work that way. Telstra, one of Australia's largest telecommunications providers, and McDonald's, one of the world's largest real estate companies (they also happen to make a really good hamburger), don't expand service or open up shop in the middle of nowhere and hope it will be profitable. Telstra reviews data from mobile phone usage in an area, internet connections, and the volume of business in the surrounding areas. Based on this data, as well whatever other information they can obtain, they decide whether to invest in a location. I am certain that McDonald's also employs its own processes to analyse an area to determine if it will get the volume of trade it required. I have found that looking carefully at these two organisations and how they deploy their resources is a low-cost way to get more information on a location, which can be quite useful in removing some of the what-ifs about a property and location.

20

Step 3. Let's Make a Deal

Once I've done my due diligence and selected a location to invest in, I look at a group of properties that fit my ideal criteria for investment. This gives me more than one option to consider, which reduces the possibility of an emotional attachment with a particular property. Aside from the block size, I prefer properties with a minimum of three bedrooms. This seems to be the ideal number of bedrooms to appeal to a broad range of renters. For instance, single people like to have space, and two extra bedrooms provides them with a second bedroom for visitors and a room that can be used as study. For young families, three bedrooms offers two rooms for children, and for just-married couples, three bedrooms allows them to expand at a later stage if they decide to have kids.

Finding a house people want to rent for the long term is great, as it's likely to be vacant for shorter periods, which means I am assured a higher return with the least amount of work. Finding these properties takes some time and effort, but once I find one, the next part is getting them for a fair price.

A place like this is a marketable property. Some people find the next step difficult: contacting the selling agent and making an offer for the property you are interested in. My friends fall into two categories: those who accept the asking price and those who haggle (I am in the category of hagglers).

I often ask my friends why they always pay the asking price. To this, I get varied responses: "I believe it was a fair price," or "I didn't have the time to haggle," or my favourite: "I know the agent, and he assured me this was the best price I could get." Here is the thing, though: Real estate agents have rules to follow, one of which is operating in the best interest of their client. This means that even if you're an agent's friend, she or he is obligated to create the best deal for the seller.

I look at the asking price as just that: the recommended price, which for me is not a fixed figure but a price the seller would be happy with. Typically, the advertised price is within a range the seller is comfortable with. It's just a question of trying to work out how big this range is and finding how far down a seller will negotiate. When I start a negotiation with a selling agent, my initial offer is usually between 15 and 20 per cent less than the asking price. In almost every instance, this first offer is knocked back; however, the counteroffer tells me how flexible the seller is. I then start a back-and-forth discussion with the agent and finally land upon a price we are all happy with.

I do several things to improve my chances of success. For instance, I try to learn as much as I can about the location. I look at the sales in the area over the past month and see what the average selling price was. I speak to leasing agents in the area, who are responsible for ensuring that tenants are reliable. They usually have a good understanding of the properties and their histories. When I know before the discussion starts whether a property has had restumping, or if the roof needs replacing, or if the plumbing has any issues, it puts me in a better position to negotiate. It also lets the agent know I've done my homework and am aware of the property's issues.

I use other bargaining chips, such as the settlement date and the subject-to-finance clause. To know how these are used, you must understand the selling agent's role and what drives them. Selling agents act on behalf of the seller; they work largely on commission, where they get a certain percentage of the sale. So the higher the sales price, the larger their commission. However, they only receive a commission after the property settles. So by offering to reduce the settlement period and removing the subject-to-finance clause, my offer can be seen as quite attractive, as it means the agent will be renumerated sooner, and there are fewer risks associated with the sale not going through.

I should point out that removing the subject-to-finance clause can be a risky proposition, as it means that if my financing falls through for any reason, I need to find an alternative way to complete the sale otherwise depending on the contract I could be liable for financial penalties.

Another way to purchase property is through an auction. I try to avoid this area. The reason is the lack of control. In an auction, you have a limited amount of time to review the property. You often can't have a building inspection, and on the day, it's you against the auctioneer, whose job is to get the most out of the crowd, and other prospective purchasers. This environment often creates a bidding frenzy.

Whilst auctions are not my preferred way to purchase, I have gone into them on a number of occasions. To prepare myself, I learn the average selling price for comparable properties in the area and determine any issues or defects with the property and location. Before the property goes up for auction, I talk to the agents and enquire about the defects or issues. I also tell the agent I'd like to buy the property and offer a price I am comfortable with. Agents are obligated to present all offers to the seller. In some cases, the seller may decide to sell to me rather than go to auction; however, more often than not, the seller will continue with to auction to see how much they can get.

I never make the opening bid at an auction. I let the auctioneer or other bidders go first. Bidding usually goes one of two ways: A number of people may place bids on a property that has a bit of interest; it's highly likely that the price will be driven up past the asking price. Or only a few bidders will be interested. I tend to go more for the ones where bidders are lean. If there is no interest, which can happen, I have an advantage, especially if I already spoke to the agent and made an initial offer. With these, I wait for the property to be passed in. At this point, I negotiate with the agent to come up with a figure that the seller and I are satisfied with.

Where there is some interest but the number of bidders is low, I tend to increase my bids in small increments. This is to wear down the other bidders. I've found that bidders at auction fall into three categories: emotional, frustrated, and experienced.

Emotional bidders are attached to the property for some reason or another. They tend to bid to the auctioneer quickly and will try to counter every other offer coming in, as if it is a personal hit upon them.

Frustrated bidders simply want the process to be over. These bidders may have experienced other auctions where they weren't successful. From what I have observed, they tend to make only a few bids, but they are high bids that try to push the other bidders out.

Experienced bidders hold back until close to the end. They are monitoring the auction to determine what the competition is like and see if the conditions are right for them to bid. Some properties don't reach the reserve price, which gives experienced bidders an edge for negotiating a deal after the auction.

Auctions are like a game of poker, in that you are dealing with people, personalities, and their body language. Emotional and frustrated bidders have tells: the look on their faces, how they respond, and so on. How I conduct myself during the auction is important. I tend to suppress any signs of emotions. I am careful with my facial expressions, body language, and speech. I am even careful with how quickly I respond. I tend to respond in a measured way and never go beyond the budget I have set.

21

Commercial Property

Like most property investors, I've bought many residential properties. However, I also invest in commercial properties. The idea for this came about when catching up with other investor friends.

When one of my friends was in his early sixties, he went through a divorce. He had a new partner, who was in her thirties. During a conversation, my friend's new partner mentioned that they were selling the properties he owned in Port Melbourne. These were considered to be blue chip properties in a sought-after area, which he had owned for a number of years and were significant assets. When she looked at them, though, she saw something different. She saw his money underperforming and encouraged him to sell these properties and free up the cash. She then directed him to a number of commercial properties in Sydney: petrol stations and shops with long-term tenancies.

The rental yield of the properties that he had in Port Melbourne were around 5.5 to 6 per cent. This was considered a good rate. However, the petrol stations and shops attracted around 10.6 per cent. This was a far better return. When I asked her about this type of setup, her response was quite interesting. She understood that residential properties were valuable but argued that the land on which the petrol stations and shops resided were also valuable; over time, they should continue to go up in value. The money coming in, though, was more than they would receive for a residential investment, which was good, as my friend was thinking about retiring soon. If that happened, negative gearing would not be an advantage to them. They needed a property investment that paid its own way and also put some money in their pockets. The other aspect she mentioned was that commercial property was simpler to manage; they had fewer issues, longer tenancies, and significantly better terms should a tenant decide to vacate. I was intrigued by these concepts, and they gave me something to think about.

I started to look at commercial properties and did some research. This category of investment included a range of property types, such as retail, industrial, multifamily, hotels, and special purpose.

Retail properties include shopping malls, individual shops, and restaurants. Industrial properties are where manufacturing and warehousing of goods occur. Multifamily buildings include high rises (whilst you may think this is a residential property, it's classed as a commercial building). Hotels are classed as a commercial structures, and finally, special purpose properties include amusement parks, churches, and self-storage facilities.

When I looked at these properties, I was attracted by the lease duration. With residential properties, lease periods were usually three, six, and twelve months. At the appropriate time, the agent would contact the tenant and determine if they wanted to stay or leave. If they stayed, great. They signed a new contract for twelve months at a similar rate, and things continued on. But if they wanted to leave, then several processes took place to ensure that the property is in the same condition as it was when the tenant started.

The property then needed to be advertised, prospective tenants had to be interviewed, and so forth. With a commercial property, you have the same type of processes, but the duration is longer. For instance, a typical tenancy can be three, five, or ten years. In addition, the contracts have more room for negotiation and often include a clause that if the tenant wishes to leave prior to the end of the contract, they are obligated to pay out the agreement in its entirety or incur a significant penalty.

Another interesting thing with a commercial property is how utilities and outgoings are managed. With residential property, the landlord pays for rates, water service charges, and inspections for appliances, as well as insurances, body corporate, and other expenditures. With a commercial property, these costs are borne by the tenant, not the landlord.

The longer tenancy periods and reduced outgoings that are borne by the landlord make a commercial property an attractive proposition. Certainly, once a house or apartment is rented, there is a certainty of income, and many outgoings are paid by the tenant. But the loans for these investments are also different. For instance, with a home loan or residential investment loan, I have a choice of interest only or interest and principal. Loan periods extend up to thirty years. With a commercial loan, the rates are higher, and the terms are shorter (generally, the loan terms are between five and twenty years). I also found that lenders have more questions, including questions around income generation from the property; this can be a problem when purchasing a new or recently constructed commercial space. Older facilities that are already rented, though, tend to be an easier sell to a lender, as they have a rental history. However, the downside with this is that if it has an established income, it usually costs more to purchase.

The logic behind this is that lending institutions place more risk on commercial loans than residential loans. This is based on the number of prospective tenants available; with residential properties, demand often outstrips supply. It's almost a certainty that a property will be rented; it's just a question of how much it's rented for. For instance, if a house is in a location with high demand, the rental price tends to be high. However, if the market or vacancy rate for a particular area is high, the landlord can simply reduce the rent to a point that it attracts a tenant, offer a shorter tenancy, or even enhance their facilities in order to attract a tenant.

Commercial properties are different, as the number of businesses requiring a space is significantly less. Also, as business models change, technology advances, and the way people work change, a number of businesses are finding they don't require a great deal of space to operate. This is even more visible as a result of Covid-19, where businesses that traditionally utilised dedicated facilities for staff to work have transitioned to a new business model, where staff can work from home and utilise a rich set of collaboration tools such as Zoom and Microsoft Teams. In addition, customers are getting used to the notion of shopping for goods and services online.

I have gone down the path of purchasing commercial property. I was attracted to the advantages this type of investment option offers. It certainly seemed to provide much more cash flow as opposed to a residential rental. But I did have concerns with this type of rental. What if the tenant vacated? What if the property didn't rent for a long period of time? What if I needed to sell the property and couldn't find a buyer? Unlike residential properties, commercial properties appeal to a smaller group of people, both on the tenant side and the investor side.

I thought about this one for some time, and the more I thought about it, the more I heard those words I hate: "What if?" I realised there was only one way I could resolve this issue, and that was by having complete control over the tenant that operated in the commercial space. To have this level of control, would allow me to be able to guide the tenant to remain in the property, to know what their outgoings and income were, and to know what their business plans were. Few businesses would provide a landlord with this level of transparency, so there was only one option that I could see.

I bought my first business in 2017. As this book is more about property, I won't go into too much detail about the purchase, but it was similar to buying a house: It involved an agent, accountants, and a solicitor to get the deal done. The business I selected was a beauty salon that specialised in nails and waxing. I chose this because it was a low-tech business, the materials required had a long shelf life, and these services would not be outmoded as a result of new technology. As for the business itself, there was a small amount of time left on its lease. This gave me a tenant who was completely predictable and willing to take out a long-term lease once I decided to purchase a commercial property.

Once I had the business, I worked to stabilise it and ensure that from a commercial perspective, it would at least break even. In the background, I also commenced looking for a new facility to purchase, in order to relocate this business to. After a few months, the agent who managed the property the salon was in wanted to commence negotiations on a new rental agreement. The owner of the property was looking to sell and wanted to ensure that they had an up-to-date lease agreement to provide a prospective buyer.

I'm not sure if this was due to luck, but it certainly was convenient. I didn't renew the lease but instead asked if the owner would accept an offer for the building prior to auction. Unfortunately, they were not taking any offers, but I was invited to attend the auction and bid if I was indeed interested in the property. I attended the auction for the property. It was one of four commercial properties being sold. I put in a few bids on this property and surprise, surprise it was one of the cheapest buildings sold that day. It was a good feeling putting in the final and winning bid for this property. But what was really good was just after the bidding had finished in front of the selling agent, whom was also the managing agent for the property, tearing up the renewal for the rental contract.

22

Step 4. Buying the Property

Not all properties are the same. Once I know what type of property I'm looking for and the location, I run the numbers to determine if it meets my requirements, and then negotiating with the real estate agent is the easy part. The area I have found to be the most tedious is the finance bit. Not so much the preapproval but the next step to go from preapproval to unconditional finance.

I have dealt with banks, building societies, and brokers, and finding the right bank and broker for me has made a difference. When I started out, I simply went to the bank where I had my everyday savings accounts, credit cards, and home loan. They were most helpful, and for the first few properties, it was an easy exercise to secure the funding I required. It was also easier to finance a deposit, as at that time, I only required a 10 per cent deposit or down payment, which was the same for home loans. However, as my investments grew, I found myself hitting a glass ceiling, which was frustrating, to say the least. The frustration was that when I did the sums, I had more than enough income to support a loan. At the time, I was told that although I had the capacity to repay the loans, the bank had certain policies in place to protect itself.

I started to shop around and found that whilst one bank said this was the case, another bank was willing to lend to me. I learnt that not all banks are equal, and the rules that one has don't necessarily apply to other banks. This factor allowed me to expand and grow my portfolio, which at that time consisted primarily of negative geared properties. However, with this particular bank, I reached a limit, due to my calculated ability to service the loan. The one trade-off with this lender was, I needed to agree to cross-collateralization; I needed to use some of the properties I already had as security, on the off chance that I ran into problems and could not repay the loan.

In hindsight, I should have thought about this more carefully, as it became somewhat restrictive for me. The first time this structure became an issue was when I started to shop around for more cost-effective loans. This was like a game of Jenga, because if I refinanced one loan, and that particular loan was for a property that was the security for another property, that meant I needed to pay down other loans to ensure that there was enough collateral.

This became an issue when I went to sell one of my properties. One of my houses had gone up significantly in value, and I wanted to take advantage of a new opportunity. So I decided to put the house on the market. It was in a good location, and within two weeks, I had an offer that provided the funds I needed and then some. However, due to cross-collateralization, some of those funds from the sale were required to reduce the bank's exposure.

Cross-collateralization is not necessarily a good or bad thing. In the early days, it enabled me to leverage my existing properties to secure loans; however, as my banking became more complex, it became an issue.

The use of brokers has been a game-changer for me. This was not something I had to do, as I was perfectly capable of approaching a lending institution directly. But there are more choices of lenders to secure funding from, and I simply didn't have the resources required to understand every possible deal and every option available to me; the market is fluctuating, and lending rules are also changing, which requires someone who is aware of the latest rules.

Selecting a broker is a personal choice; what works for me might not necessarily work for you. You are dealing with a person who is acting on your behalf to secure the best deal for you. Most brokers listen to their client and do their best to give them what they need, but it's important to remember that brokers have alliances with certain lenders. They are able to cut better deals with the lenders they have an alliance with. In situations where they don't have an alliance, they can contact another broker, who has a relationship with the lending institution you are looking to deal with, and between the two of them, you'll get the result you require.

There was a real learning curve in understanding what it is that I need in a broker. I didn't need someone who regurgitates data that is in the news, nor do I need them to provide me with information that is too specific. What I need is someone who understands my goals, knows how I want to grow my portfolio, and has a tenacity for getting things done. My current broker fits this criteria perfectly. They work with me, provide guidance on what is available in the market, and know what levels of income I need to generate. This enables me to focus on finding a property and gives me the confidence I need to cut the most aggressive deals possible.

Here is an example of a broker being a personal choice: Two of my friends asked me to recommend a broker. One of my friends owned his own home as well as an investment property. The other friend was new to the country, but also new to the property market; he and his wife were looking to buy their first home. As my primary broker specialised in residential lending, I recommended my primary broker to both of my friends and didn't think too much about it.

A month later, I heard back from both friends. My first friend was so thankful for the recommendation, as my broker had managed to secure them a more competitive rate with another lender; the broker also leveraged some of the deals from the lenders, which resulted in the refinancing process putting a few thousand dollars extra into my friend's pocket.

My other friend, though, wasn't so happy. When I asked why, he said they weren't returning their messages, and he felt that given the value of the loan, they expected more hand-holding. This concerned me, as it certainly didn't seem like the way my broker would operate; however, brokers are bound by privacy laws, so I couldn't ask them about it. I decided to ask my friend a few more questions.

My friend told my broker they need preapproval urgently, so they could look for a property. My broker obtained their income details, advised them what level of finance they could obtain, and provided a few lending institutions to consider; the broker then recommended my friend proceed with applying for preapproval, as that would enable them to get more accurate data on rates and fees. However, my friend wanted to know all the rates and fees before they applied for preapproval. It was a bit chicken-and-egg; however, after some discussion, my friend understood that in order to get the information he wanted, he needed to sign an application form, which he did, and a few days later, he had the information he needed.

Preapproval is only the first step, and it certainly doesn't mean that everything is done and dusted. It mean that some of the basic metrics banks use to measure if a deal works for them are met and, if so, how much they are willing to lend. I have experienced that every lender is different; they ask different questions and seek different amounts of information. I've been asked to submit the following:

- payslips
- bank statements

- employment contracts
- rental statements
- outline of living expenses
- current property valuation reports

Most lenders ask for this information. In some instances, I have chosen a smaller lender because they offered more services than the larger banks. What I have experienced, though, is whilst the offers or deal can be better, the lender tends to be a bit more cautious and ask more questions. For example, I have been asked to provide certificate of currency for all properties. I've also had to submit the following:

- explanation of why I prefer a particular type of job over another
- twenty-four months of bank statements
- tax returns for the previous two years
- letters from my accountant attesting to my ability to service a loan
- interim business statements
- a statement from my work's HR department attesting to my employment
- letters from managing director of my employer confirming their need for my services

Some of these questions are understandable, but others can seem on the tedious side. But the way I see it is, each time a bank lends me money, it takes a risk on my ability to repay the loan. So if this is what they need to do in order to be comfortable with lending to me, then so be it.

I learnt many lessons from Robert Kiyosaki's book *Rich Dad, Poor Dad*. This book touched on living within your means and described how his rich father didn't always purchase the latest and greatest things but simply bought the things they needed. By following the same approach, when a bank looks at my statements, they can see the hallmarks of good saving practices. My statements include very few items such as takeaway, dinning out, or retail therapy. The bank sees income coming in and bills being paid on time. The other thing they see is that my credit card, whilst having a number of transactions on it, has zero interest charged on it consistently. In fact, one time, interest of $106 was charged on my card, but this was a banking error, and it was reversed.

Once I go through a preapproval process, if it's successful, that is a green light for me to search for a property that meets my requirements. Whether it's positively or negatively geared, I place a deposit on the property. This is when things start to get real as I move from preapproval to what is called unconditional approval. In order to get unconditional approval, the lender asks for more detail and requests the data I mentioned previously. To protect myself, when I put in an offer, in the contract if I don't have a plan b standing by for alternative funding that is when I stipulate that it is subject to finance and contingent on a building inspection. So if the lender decides not to approve, or there is an issue with the property I didn't pick up initially, I can still get out of the contract. This is an important step, as some contracts are written so that once you sign, you are committed to buying the property.

At the same time the lender is doing their due diligence, I look for a conveyancer in the same state as the property I am purchasing. The laws for property purchases in Australia vary from state to state. So by choosing a local conveyancer, I can be sure they understand the rules of that particular state. I ask all my conveyancers if they support Property Exchange Australia (PEXA). This is actually the world's first online lodgement and financial settlement platform, which has been around since 2017. This platform is not mandatory in every state, but more and more conveyancers and banks are adopting this service. What I like about this service is the speed and efficiency of this solution. Prior to PEXA, settlements would require the exchanging of physical documents. This would mean that documents would need to be taken to a common location by both conveyance groups, witnessed, exchanged, and lodged with the land and titles office in whichever state a property was being purchased. In addition, cheques would need to be drawn and deposited into each respective bank. This process could take several days to finalise. In contrast, PEXA creates a portal that allows banks and conveyancers to collaborate in real time; they carry out a settlement and then use electronic transfers to send the appropriate funds to the right location, which results in same-day settlement.

The final step is to take out insurance for the property prior to settlement. This removes the risk of anything happening to the property as it settles, and it's something that a number of banks ask to see in place before allowing funds to transfer.

23

Step 5. Running the Property

Once a property has been settled, it's not the end of the story. Running the property takes a little bit of effort. I mentioned earlier in the book my main levers are insurance, loan repayments, and rental returns. But there are other aspects to look at:

- water charges
- tax rates
- managing agents
- deductions

Some of these costs are fixed, but others can vary. For instance, rental returns can vary, simply by setting a higher price when the lease period is up. Also, loan repayments can vary, based on sourcing the best deal. I also look at my deductions; I have three areas that I focus on: deductions for improvements on a property, deductions for depreciation, and deductions for any repairs that need to be carried out.

I'll start with deductions for improvements. When I am about to purchase a property, I look for opportunities to add immediate value. For instance, items like solar panels, split systems, new carpet, and new kitchen appliances can add more value to a property. In the big scheme of things, paint is cheap, but there is something about a freshly painted property, both inside and outside, which can completely change a house's look; it seems more modern and helps make it more appealing to prospective tenants.

This does a couple of things. Firstly, it gives the agent I choose to work with a more marketable property; they can often secure a higher rent as a result of these additions. It can also add items which can be depreciated while boosting the value of the property. I keep a complete list of these changes, along with my invoices and receipts, which I pass over to my accountant.

The next step is to bring in someone to review the property and create a depreciation schedule. I only do this once for a property, and I try to do it after I've made all the planned improvements. This gives my accountant a complete list of what items can be depreciated, as well as an indication on how much value to depreciate over a period. There is quite a bit of literature on the internet about depreciation, as well as when to and when not to have a depreciation schedule carried out. The Australian Tax Office made a ruling which prohibited accountants from estimating the construction costs of a property if it was built after 1985.

Whilst I do have properties that fit into this criteria, as well as houses that are significantly older than this, I still carry out a depreciation schedule for all my properties. This gives my accountant the most accurate information; instead of guessing the value of items, they can base a deduction on actual data from a qualified surveyor who has visited the facility. Also, the report itself and the cost incurred can be deducted, so I see it as a win-win.

The final costs are deductions for repairs and maintenance. I mentioned earlier in this book that I put a small portion of my rent into an offset account for repairs and maintenance. Whilst this is simplistic, it works for me; I typically keep enough in there to pay for the majority of issues that occur. For anything more substantial, that's where my insurance comes into play.

Issues that come up fall into two categories: those that need to be fixed immediately and those that can wait. For instance, an electrical fault or blocked plumbing needs immediate attention. But a squeaky door or damaged fly screen, whilst important, can wait a few days to do. For the immediate repairs, my agents are allowed to have the work carried out, up to a certain discretionary figure, after which they need to seek my approval to go further.

This ensures that I am not woken up in the middle of the night for something that requires attention. As for the repairs that can wait, even though I know I can deduct them, as a matter of good practice, I ask my agents to provide me with multiple quotes for the work. This does a couple of things; firstly, it ensures that the costs are reasonable. Secondly, it allows me to become familiar with the tradespeople in the area, which can be useful for any future needs. Yes, I know I could simply use Hipages or Airtasker or another website to find tradespeople; they are a great resource, and I have used them in the past. However, having information about tradespeople who are reliable and have experience maintaining rental properties can really make a difference.

I tend to keep contact info on three types of trades in a location: general handyman, plumber, and electrician. Having access to these types of tradespeople helps ensure that the day-to-day maintenance issues can be dealt with in a quick, efficient, and cost-effective manner.

These are some of the key maintenance works that I bring these people in to do:

- annual smoke alarm checks
- gas appliance checks
- guttering repairs and maintenance
- patching of defects in plaster

- sanding of doors that may have dropped or expanded
- unblocking pipes that have obstructions

The next area I focus on is the agent. I have heard some horror stories from friends and family who had a tenant leave, only to find they left a substantial mess that is costly to take care off. Someone I know was left with a bill of around forty thousand dollars and needed to have a complete bathroom refit after a tenant left.

Over the past ten years, I've only had one instance where a tenant decided to leave a property with a considerable amount of rubbish, a few holes in a wall, and essentially a space that needed work before it could be rented again. I visited the property and was greeted with an unpleasant smell in the living and kitchen, a garage full of junk, and a backyard that was full of cigarette butts. Suffice to say, the tenant didn't get their bond back, and it required money out of my repairs and maintenance funds to be rented again.

When I hear stories about where something has gone wrong with a property, I normally hear that the tenant was terrible and left the property like one of those break rooms where you are given a sledgehammer and told to go wild and break whatever you can. In other instances, I hear that the landlord is terrible and does not respond to normal requests in a reasonable amount of time. These stories may all be valid, but I often wonder where the agent was in these situations. After all, they were appointed by the landlord to represent them and were the point of contact for the tenant.

I spoke with my agent who was looking after the place where I had a problem; he told me he had problems getting in contact with the tenant; each time he wanted to view the property, the tenant was out, so he wasn't able to carry out the inspection. I thought this response was odd; more than that, I thought it was a cop-out, as the agent was the one who found, reviewed, and recommended the tenant. In addition, the contract the tenant signed said they agreed to having four inspections carried out per annum. So by not allowing this, they were in breach. But instead of sorting this out, the agent skipped an inspection for a quarter.

This particular agent no longer manages property for me. I insist that my agents provide quarterly inspection reports, with date-stamped photos. This allows me to see the house's condition and also ensures that the agent is actively managing the property. I treat my agents like my insurance and loan providers. I review them annually to gauge their performance. Some are definitely better than others; these are the criteria I use to measure an agent:

- level of detail on inspection reports
- number of issues escalated to me for a property
- number of rental properties under management
- management fees
- retenanting fees
- date-stamps on the photos in the inspection reports
- Google reviews of the agents

This process of constant review has worked to find agents who are increasingly better, not only from a money perspective but from a quality of service. This in turn also leads to better quality tenants, more detailed quarterly property inspections, as well as better information on the rental market in the area.

24

Where to Next?

In 2010, when I purchased my first investment property, it was a journey into the unknown. I always had an interest in this type of investment, but I had no idea just how much it would change the way I looked at property, architecture, and renovating. I enjoy the process of getting my finances in order, working with brokers, negotiating with agents, and finding properties that suit my needs. I feel a sense of pride that even with limited finances, a home mortgage, kids in school, and all the other expenses that are part of living, I have managed to push the envelope of what I thought was possible.

I now have seventeen properties working for me, providing me with cash flow, ongoing wealth, and a passive income which will only grow stronger over time, as the loans on the properties burn down.

Do I feel rich? Well, no. I have some wealth behind me now, and I certainly feel that I am in a far better position than I was in after the GFC, with more options available to me and a better tolerance to endure periods without a day job. But I also have considerable debts to pay off; however, they are good debts instead of bad debts. I still drive a second-hand car, I still check the prices of everything I buy, and I still consider carefully where every dollar I earn goes.

This book contains stories, information, and my thoughts on property investment. The one true thing I have learnt about property is that there are so many different ways to invest, so many new ideas, so many ways of doing things. After all this time, I am still learning.

In hindsight, I could have been more aggressive with my property investment; I could have followed the buy, renovate, and flip approach to generate an income stream. Or I could have started to invest in property earlier. But I took the path I felt was right for me and invested when the time and motivation worked for me. Investment of any kind does come with risk. What if it doesn't work? What if I can't afford it? What if my circumstances change at some point? These are all valid questions, but so too is What if I do nothing? If I was to do nothing, then nothing would have been the result, so I chose to try something and see where it would take me. As for what's next, I am still on the journey and always looking for my next property. I also find a great amount of joy imparting knowledge and information to people and seeing them get results and improve their financial position.

To you, the reader: you have made it to the final paragraph. I thank you for reading my book and hope you found it interesting and useful. If there is one thing that I can impart to you, it is no matter where in the world you are and what type of investment you are considering, the key is to get as much information as you can, weigh up the what if's, and if you believe it will work, then listen to that little voice inside that says, "Shut up and do it."

www.ingramcontent.com/pod-product-compliance
Lightning Source LLC
Chambersburg PA
CBHW021435210526
45463CB00002B/527